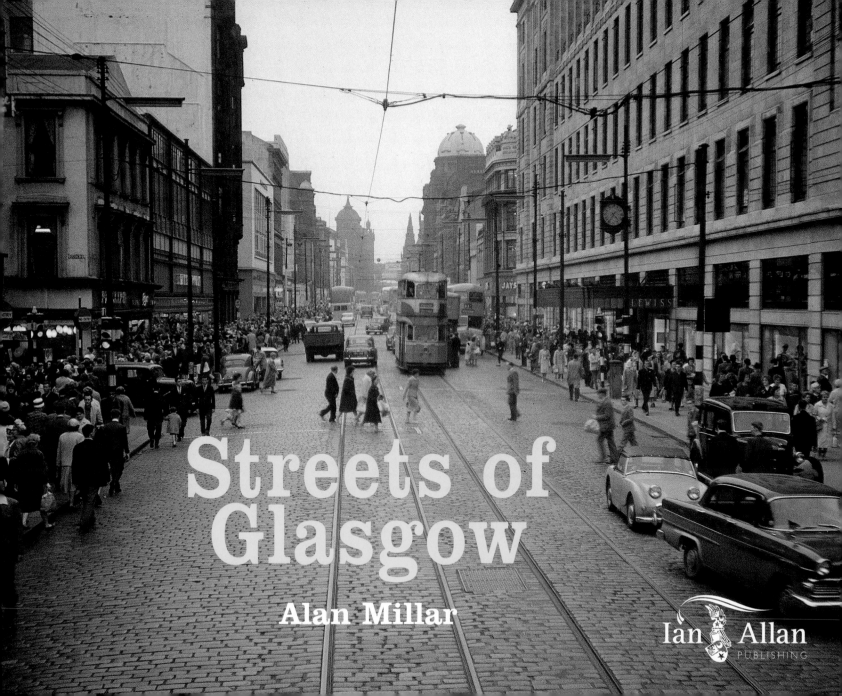

Streets of Glasgow

Alan Millar

Ian Allan
PUBLISHING

Introduction

One of many old sayings about my home city is that Glasgow made the River Clyde and the Clyde made Glasgow. It would not have become a thriving seaport and centre of shipbuilding had it not been built on a west-flowing river, and the river brought that prosperity only through the vision of Glasgow's merchants and the labours of its populace.

You could compose a similar tale of interdependence between the city and its public transport, especially of the trams that were an integral part of its streetscape from August 1872 to September 1962. Glasgow claimed that its was the world's finest tramway system. Even if others could challenge that civic boast, in its heyday this system was certainly among the most comprehensive and efficient in the developed world. It provided cheap, frequent transport to most parts of the city — middle-class as well as working-class — catering for workers, shoppers, students and pleasure-seekers. It helped shape the city's streets. Yet those streets also contributed towards the success of the trams, for Glasgow embraced the Scottish tradition of building upwards rather than outwards, accommodating most of its pre-World War 1 population in sandstone tenement flats built within three to four miles of the city centre. Those often overcrowded flats were seldom more than a couple of minutes' walk from the nearest tram stop, so it was far easier for a tramway to be efficient and profitable when most of its customers were clustered so close together.

As late as 1600, Glasgow was a sleepy university town with a population estimated at no more than 7,000. There were 10 larger towns on Scotland's east coast. But the 1707 union with England provided its ambitious merchants with access to new colonial markets, especially in the West Indies and North America. Its population topped 100,000 in 1811, was nudging 500,000 when the first tram ran 61 years later and exceeded 760,000 in 1901.

Money was little object to Glasgow's Victorians, who splashed out on flamboyant public architecture and followed an American-style grid system for most city-centre streets. They also believed in municipal provision of water, gas, electricity, telephones, public parks, museums and art galleries and improving the quality of housing. Hardly surprising, then, that Glasgow Corporation took over the tramway system in July 1894. Within eight years, horses were replaced by electric traction. It built most of its own tramcars and enlarged the system to reach beyond the city boundaries.

Glasgow's population topped one million after annexing the riverside burghs of Partick and Govan in November 1912 and peaked at 1.3 million during World War 2. However, the post-World War 1 city was different and less confident. Heavy industry was in decline, the city's politics became more volatile, and the tenement-building boom was over. Lower-density housing with individual gardens came into favour — some built by private developers, much more of it by the Corporation — and the size of the city more than doubled as it swallowed up more green fields and small villages in 1926, 1931 and 1938 to provide land for new homes. The Corporation also acquired the adjoining Airdrie & Coatbridge and Paisley District tramways in 1922 and 1923, the cable-hauled Glasgow District Subway railway in 1923 and ran its first motor buses late the following year. However, the new suburbs didn't lend

Previous page: Looking east along Argyle Street on Saturday 1 September 1962, the last day of normal operation of Glasgow's once massive tramway service. In this view from an eastbound tram, pedestrians throng the pavements while 'Cunarder' 1358, then a mere 12 years old, loads outside Lewis's (now Debenham's) department store on service 9, the last British city tram route until Manchester's Metrolink started in 1992. A less-than-two-years-old Corporation Leyland Titan PD3/2 collects its passengers from the kerbside. Until June 1961 trams provided the only public transport along Argyle Street and Trongate. This section, between Queen Street and Glassford Street, was pedestrianised in July 1976. *Iain MacGregor*

First published 2004

ISBN 0 7110 2994 6

Published by Ian Allan Publishing

an imprint of Ian Allan Publishing Ltd, Hersham, Surrey KT12 4RG.
Printed by Ian Allan Printing Ltd, Hersham, Surrey KT12 4RG.

Code: 0402/B1

themselves as readily to tramways as they did to the new fangled, more flexible buses and a complementary network of cross-city routes grew up from the mid-1920s.

To protect itself against competition from private bus operators — many destined to become part of the Scottish Motor Traction group (later the state-owned Scottish Bus Group) — the Corporation secured Parliamentary powers in 1930 that prevented other operators from carrying local passengers within the boundaries as they applied then, although the other operators could run buses in the 10,216 acres added to Glasgow in 1931 and 1938. The boundary restriction added to the number and variety of buses serving the city, but it also frustrated intending passengers — especially those who, on a wet Sunday afternoon, waited in vain for a Corporation service while red, blue or green SMT or SBG buses sped past in the very direction in which they intended to travel.

While many other cities scrapped their trams in the 1930s, Glasgow invested in new trams and routes, but the tide turned dramatically after World War 2. Government policy moved 250,000 Glaswegians to East Kilbride, Cumbernauld, Livingston, Glenrothes and Irvine new towns and to 60 other communities across Scotland. The huge postwar peripheral council housing schemes at Drumchapel, Easterhouse and Castlemilk absorbed

another 100,000 within the extended city boundaries, while a further 250,000 were rehoused within 29 comprehensive development areas of new low- and high-rise housing. Added to that upheaval, a network of urban motorways, expressways, tunnels and high-level bridges was to separate traffic from people and buildings. There was talk of a new light-rapid-transit network, but instead the nationalised British Transport Commission persuaded the authorities to invest in electrified 'heavy' railways. The Corporation was manœuvred into abandoning most services beyond the city boundaries, where BTC's buses took their place.

Between 1949 and 1958 the Corporation invested in 195 trolleybuses, but motor buses replaced the bulk of the tram network between 1957 and 1962, and the trolleybuses lasted for only five years after the trams. Over that same period

Above: If Glasgow has a signature Victorian skyline, then this is part of it. Glasgow University, the neo-Gothic work of English architect Sir George Gilbert Scott, is at the top left, while the three Italianate towers of the former Trinity College (now apartments) and (next to the crane) J. T. Rochead's Park Church tower stand alongside the mid-19th-century terraces of Woodlands Hill. In this February 1970 view (recorded from offices in India Street) a Corporation Leyland Atlantean on service 32 heads along North Street and passes the Mitchell Library — Scotland's largest reference library and one of the largest in Europe — which relocated here in 1911. Behind it are the ruins of the St Andrew's Halls (a concert and boxing venue) which burned down in October 1962 and into which the library has since expanded. The western flank of the M8 inner-ring motorway is well advanced. *Brian Deans*

The final extension of the Glasgow tramway system — the half-mile from Knightswood Cross west along the central median of the Great Western Road 'Boulevard' to the Forth & Clyde Canal bridge at Blairdardie — opened on 31 July 1949. This development in the outer western suburbs occurred five months after motor buses (later trolleybuses) replaced the High Street trams. It also marked the final extension of any first-generation British tramway system. At the time, Corporation Transport Manager Eric R. L. Fitzpayne was proposing the development of a light rapid-transit system, with articulated single-deck trams using the centres of dual carriageways as well as under-employed rail trackbed and new tunnels. There also were plans for a further mile-and-three-quarters westward extension from Blairdardie to Duntocher, but this was never built, and Duntocher lost its only trams in December 1949, when buses replaced them on the single-deck shuttle service to Clydebank and Yoker.

The Blairdardie extension survived for fewer than 11 years and was grassed over after tram 30 was withdrawn in March 1960. In this view looking south-west, three service 30 'Standard' trams are on the reserved tramway, with the rightmost waiting at the end of the line next to the canal, visible above the newly built white flats. Multi-storey flats were built later on the open space on the opposite side of the canal. An AEC Regent III on route 33 is climbing Blairdardie Road in front of the school in the foreground, while two Corporation double-deckers are on the Boulevard to the right, beyond the tram terminus. The chimneys towards the top left are at Yoker power station, the two tall electricity pylons to its left are either side of the Clyde at Renfrew Ferry, and the cranes near the top right are in the John Brown shipyard at Clydebank. *Jim Thomson*

4

the Corporation, SBG and private operators provided buses to the new housing schemes, and in 1973 the Greater Glasgow (later Strathclyde) Passenger Transport Executive took over the Corporation's buses and underground railway (these days once again called the Subway).

This book looks at how Glasgow and its public transport changed between 1951 and the early 1970s — years when trams faded out of the city's life, when trolleybuses flourished briefly, bus conductors were phased out and buses appeared with engines under the floor or in a box at the back. These also were years when many familiar communities were erased from the face of Glasgow's earth along with their shops, pubs, cinemas, dance halls, factories and docks. Yet, for all that has changed, much also remains familiar. In part, we can thank the lobbyists and decision-makers who stalled the most devastating road schemes still being mooted in the early 1970s and those who recognised — before it was too late — that solid, refurbished and stone-cleaned tenements offered better housing conditions than many of the tower blocks built so hurriedly in the 1960s; also those who axed a sixth new town planned for Stonehouse in Lanarkshire and turned their attention instead to Glasgow. Their faith and persistence and the city's rediscovery of its self-worth has revived its inner core, with smart new offices, new and refurbished central area housing, vibrant restaurants and a growing bus service all symptoms of better times.

The pictures that follow progress from the city centre through the western, northern, eastern and southern districts. As you look at them, be grateful that men now mostly in their late 50s, 60s, 70s or older — and some sadly no longer with us — had the foresight and enthusiasm to photograph the scenes of 30 to 50 years ago, of trams, buses and trolleybuses in urban settings so ordinary then, yet of a different age, when retail chains were the exception, when men and women wore hats, when jackets, ties and gabardine macs counted as leisure wear, prams were constructed like tanks and such car traffic as existed was British-built. I'm immensely grateful to all for the trouble they have taken in looking out suitable slides and for their trust in lending them to me. All are acknowledged alongside their photographs. Special thanks, however, go to Phil Tatt for making this one of his first priorities on return from hospital following a serious illness and to Brian Patton, Alistair Gunn and Roger Jones of the Light Rail Transit Association for unlocking the treasure-trove of pictures taken by the late Jack Wyse and Frank Hunt in the early 1950s. Copies of the Colour-Rail tram pictures (and many more like them) are available from 5 Treacher's Close, Chesham, Bucks, HP5 2HD, quoting the reference numbers (where shown) in the appropriate captions. Photobus also sells prints and slides of buses, trolleybuses and trams in Glasgow.

The information that accompanies the pictures came from a wide variety of published sources. Those that were especially useful were the Scottish Tramway Museum (now Tramway & Transport) Society's *The Glasgow Tramcar* (Ian G. McM. Stewart), *A Handbook of Glasgow Tramways* (D. L. Thomson), *Glasgow Trolleybuses* (Brian T. Deans) and *A Handbook of Glasgow Corporation Motorbuses* (Stuart M. Little), The PSV Circle and the Omnibus Society's fleet history of Glasgow Corporation Transport, and two general historic reference books, Blackie's *The Second City* (C. A. Oakley) and Mainstream Publishing's *The Glasgow Encyclopædia* (Joe Fisher).

Finally, special thanks are due to my West Midlands-born wife, Barbara, not only for her forbearance while this book consumed what should have been leisure hours but also for sharing her knowledge as a tour guide working in this wonderful city.

Alan Millar
Glasgow, December 2003

Left: Glasgow's trams may have disappeared over 40 years ago, but significant traces remain. Besides the trams preserved in the city's own transport museum and elsewhere, several bus routes run largely where trams preceded them for decades. But the most visible traces — on countless city tenement buildings — are the rosettes fixed in their sandstone walls to support overhead wires. This one is in Pollokshields, with a plate next to the street name reminding us of the London-style postal districts that Glasgow used before postcodes appeared in the early 1970s. S1 became G41. *Alan Millar*

Left: The Georgians and Victorians expanded Glasgow westwards, and George Square — laid out in 1781 and named after King George III, who had come to the throne 21 years earlier — is today's city centre. This is the southeastern corner, with Corporation trolleybus TB112 turning into South Frederick Street on the city's last trolleybus route, the 105 from Queen's Cross to Muirend and Clarkston. Twelve statues adorn the square, with the novelist Sir Walter Scott atop the central column behind the trolley booms. The other statues include Queen Victoria, but there is none to George III, whose loss of the American colonies in 1776 made him unpopular with Glasgow's hitherto wealthy tobacco merchants. The tower on the far left is part of the Merchant's House, designed by noted Glasgow architect John Burnet and built 1874-7. A merchant ship in full sail is atop the dome. TB112 was one of 90 Crossley- and Park Royal-bodied BUT 9613Ts new in 1957/8 and is in the livery worn by most of Glasgow's trolleybuses from 1953 until the system closed in 1967. The colours were the same as those carried by motor buses until 1965, but with green where motor buses had cream, and cream between the decks instead of green; this was to hide the dirt caused by a build-up of carbon dirt from their trolley booms. Most trolleybuses had green rather than black destination blinds. TB, by the way, stood not for 'Trolley Bus' but for 'Trolleybus BUT'. There also were TD, TG and TBS classes. *Ian Stewart*

Above: The women waiting for two Corporation AEC Regents to pass them in the northwestern corner of George Square in July 1965 must surely subscribe to the words of Oscar Hammerstein II and believe that brown paper packages tied up with string — from the days before shops provided plastic carrier bags — are one of their favourite things. A23 — freshly repainted with crimson lake wheels, lifeguards and front springs — is one of 50 Crossley-bodied Regent IIIs new in 1948/9 and is being followed by one of 89 Regent Vs new 1960-2 with forward-entrance Alexander bodywork. The core part of route 6, which from 1938 connected the inter-war suburbs of Garscadden in the west and Provanmill the east, was operating by 1929. The North British (now Millennium) Hotel is in the foreground and has since been extended across the entrance to Queen Street railway station, the NB Railway's Glasgow terminal of 1842. Part of the station's 170ft glass roof span is just visible above A23. The Gothic-columned building behind the Regent V is the former West George Street Independent Church, built in 1818, acquired by the Edinburgh & Glasgow Railway Company in 1848, converted to offices in 1856 and demolished in 1975. Today the site is occupied by Consort House, headquarters of Strathclyde Passenger Transport. *Iain MacGregor*

Westbound 'Coronation' tram 1275 and a 'Cunarder' in the Trongate, just west of Glasgow Cross, the old centre of the city. The steeple to the left is all that remains of the Tolbooth, the 1626 town hall, courthouse and prison. The tall building above the following trams is the Mercat Building of 1922, while the low building (with part of a Red Hackle whisky advertisement visible behind tram 1275) is Glasgow Cross station on the Central low-level railway, which opened in November 1895. Closed in October 1964, the line was electrified and reopened in November 1979, but this station, demolished two years earlier, was replaced by the new Argyle Street station, a few blocks farther west. The Capstan advertisement to the right of the Mercat Building is on one of the bridges of the City of Glasgow Union Railway. No 1275 was one of 152 broadly similar 64-seat bogie trams built in the Corporation's workshops between 1936 and 1941. It operated from January 1940 until June 1962, and its *Evening Citizen* advertisement for a 'Bombs on the Clyde' feature suggests that this is 1961, the 20th anniversary of the March 1941 Clydebank Blitz, in which this tram was severely damaged. Following a fire in 1957, it was rebuilt with flush-fitting windows similar to those on six further 'Coronations' built in 1954. *Ian Stewart*

Right: Daimler CTM6 trolleybus TD1 heads south through Glasgow Cross from the High Street to Saltmarket in May 1951, with the Tolbooth steeple behind. The curved roadway to the left carries northbound traffic and was created when the West Quadrant buildings behind were built in 1920. Plans for an East Quadrant were never realised, and, happily, the city eventually lifted a serious threat to drive an eastern flank of the inner ring motorway through this historic area in the early 1970s. Glasgow University was in the High Street from 1451 until it moved to the West End in 1870. Trolleybuses served the High Street and Saltmarket from the start of operations in April 1949 until April 1966. This is the first route, the 102, which replaced tram service 2 between Riddrie and Polmadie; the 101 to Shawfield started in November 1949 and was extended to Rutherglen in February 1956. TD1, with 70-seat Metro-Cammell body to London Transport design, shows the livery applied to the first 64 trolleybuses when they were new in 1949/50 but which was phased out by 1956. Only the 30 Daimlers carried the city's coat of arms and 'Let Glasgow Flourish' motto on the upper panels, and this was moved to the green panels to make way for advertisements. The drawback of this livery was its inability to conceal carbon dirt from the trolley booms; during 1951 the Corporation began painting their roofs green after experimenting with brown and grey, then adopted the mainly green livery shown on page 10. *W. J. Wyse collection / LRTA London Area*

Right : Southbound single-deck trolleybus TBS4 at the foot of the 'Bell o' the Brae' farther up the High Street in 1956, while operating service 102. The Corporation ran few single-deck buses or trams, using them mainly for odd routes with obstacles to higher vehicles. However, it bought 11 of these BUT RETB1s in 1950 and 1953 to test the Continental European practice of providing sufficient seats (27 on TBS4) for passengers riding outside the peak periods but standing room only for another 40 (reduced to 30 in 1955) at busy times. Passengers boarded by a rear door and paid a seated conductor who sat behind a counter — just as a supermarket checkout assistant might today. On the first of these buses, they left by an exit next to the driver, but the 10 — like TBS4 — bodied by East Lancs in 1953 instead had a wider exit nearer the middle. Perhaps because there were so few of them, they were not considered successful and by 1955 were relegated largely to peak-hour duties. They were later rebuilt with just one door, more seats and room for just eight standing passengers, and were staffed by a roving conductor. All were taken out of service in 1964 and scrapped the following year. In this view, the Continental Tours shop has been vacated by Cotter's, a long-established coach business that survived until the mid-1980s, following its move to Buchanan Street. *Frank Hunt collection / LRTA London Area*

Left: This is the top of the High Street on 30 April 1966, the day before motor-bus route 27 replaced the 101/102 trolleybuses. TB18, in the spray-painted livery in which most of these buses were repainted after 1960 and with its redundant 'via' destination display panelled over, is crossing the top of John Knox Street at Cathedral Square. This is where Glasgow began in the sixth century. On the left, beyond the new Austin 1100 saloon, is Provand's Lordship, Glasgow's oldest dwelling house. It dates from 1471 and was originally the manse of the master or preceptor of the adjacent chapel and hospital of St Nicholas, the ruins of which were demolished in the early 19th century. To the right are the 1904-14 Royal Infirmary buildings, which survive today. Much else has changed in this part of town: the 1993 Scots-baronial-style St Mungo Museum of Religious Life & Art stands on the open square in front of the infirmary, Strathclyde University campus occupies much of the area around Provand's Lordship, while the buildings in the distance were swept away by the M8 motorway. The 27 bus has also long since vanished into history. *Iain MacGregor*

Right: Another scene from the last day of the High Street trolleybuses, with TB14 heading south across the Albert Bridge, built in 1871 to link Saltmarket with Crown Street on the south side of the Clyde. The Justiciary Court House is to the left of the bus. Two Central SMT Bristol Lodekkas are behind, one following TB14 southwards, the other heading for Glasgow Cross and Gallowgate. Buses no longer serve either the Albert Bridge or Saltmarket and run instead via Trongate to reach Stockwell Street and the St Enoch shopping centre. *Alistair Gunn*

Central SMT H46, a 1951 Guy Arab III with lowbridge Guy bodywork, in the eastern end of Clyde Street in 1966 on the last leg of its journey from Wishaw to Waterloo Street bus station. It is passing the French-style fish market of 1873, which was converted into an arts centre and retail gallery in 1985/6 before sadly once again falling out of use. The bridge dates from 1899 and carries the under-used City of Glasgow Union Railway, which has the potential one day to connect the lines south of the city with the Queen Street low-level system and possibly to lines serving the east and north of Scotland. The bridge, which replaced an 1870 structure, also carried trains into St Enoch station until it closed in June 1966. The Central bus in the distance is HR1, one of two rear-engined Leyland Atlanteans taken over in 1961 with the Hamilton-based Chieftain business and operated on East Kilbride–Glasgow routes until they were sold in 1969. *Robert Grieves*

Right: A newer Central SMT bus, 1967 Leyland Leopard T35 with Alexander Y-type bodywork, bound for Shotts along the Bridgegate — or 'Briggait', as it's known to most — which parallels Clyde Street and extends from the Victoria Bridge to the Saltmarket. The Victoria Wire Works advertisement points to one of the city's smallest streets. Goosedubs — which survives as the name of a footpath running off Stockwell Street — earned its name because one Provost Aird allowed his flock of geese to splash in the puddles or 'dubs' here. The name isn't unique though, for Edinburgh still has a Guse Dubs. The Leopard is typical of hundreds bought by the Scottish Bus Group between 1963 and 1982 — as are the paper destination bills in its windscreen. *Alan Millar*

Below right: This view of the Victoria Bridge (site of Glasgow's first, 14th-century stone bridge over the Clyde) was taken from a northbound tram in May 1951. The Western SMT Leyland Titan PD2/1 with highbridge Northern Counties body is one of around 130 buses taken over in 1950/1 when the British Transport Commission acquired Scotland's then largest independent bus company, Young's of Paisley. It is turning out of Carlton Place to reach its terminus in Clyde Street, alongside the wharves on the opposite bank. It's advertising King's of Wishaw, a company whose Oddfellows and other boiled sweets no doubt helped keep West of Scotland dentists in National Health Service fees and whose equipment is preserved in the Summerlee Industrial Museum in Coatbridge. Two mounted police are riding south over the bridge while a Corporation Standard tram heads towards Stockwell Street. The tenements and warehouses on Clyde Street have been demolished and partly replaced by modern apartments. *W. J. Wyse collection / LRTA London Area*

Glasgow's magistrates controlled the proliferation of private bus operators after World War 1 by designating certain streets as compulsory termini — or, to use that peculiarly Scottish term, stances — from February 1926. The western section of Clyde Street between Glasgow and Victoria bridges, Carlton Place (on the opposite bank) and Adelphi Street (across the river from the fishmarket) were among the streets treated effectively as open-air bus stations. Western SMT and, to a lesser extent, Central SMT continued to use Clyde Street until the new Anderston bus station opened in February 1971. The wharf buildings were then swept away, and a landscaped riverside walkway deservedly won awards for urban renewal. Sadly, it has fallen into disrepair. In this August 1964 view, Western SMT MD488, a lowbridge all-Leyland Titan PD1 of 1947, waits between journeys while a Central SMT Titan stands behind with the fishmarket roof behind that. The queue opposite is waiting for Central buses coming from Waterloo Street bus station. The Western SMT bus displays merely a destination, as the company did not introduce service numbers until the mid-1950s.
Campbell Sayers

Western's services to Renfrew, Gourock and Largs departed from North Drive, the vehicular approach ramp to St Enoch station. The London, Midland & Scottish Railway, which inherited the station — opened in 1876 and enlarged in 1898 — from the Glasgow & South Western Railway in the 1923 Grouping, owned buses on these routes between 1929 and 1931. The 204ft span of the station's glass roof looms behind Inchinnan-based Leyland Titan PD3A/3 ID1665 as it emerges from Maxwell Street to turn right into Clyde Street in 1964 on its short journey to Paisley North. Its lowbridge Alexander bodywork

was among the last built for the Scottish Bus Group with an awkward offside sunken gangway and four-abreast seating upstairs. After it closed, St Enoch station was used as a city-centre car park until 1977, when it was demolished to make way for a planned new Ministry of Defence headquarters; its stonework (and that of many demolished tenements) helped fill in the Queen's Dock. The MoD relocation plan came to naught, however, and in 1989 the St Enoch Shopping Centre — then Europe's largest glass-covered mall — opened on this site. *Campbell Sayers*

St Enoch Square in 1959, with rail travellers using the stairs leading to the station entrance on the vehicle ramp above. The large red sign hanging from the lamp-post next to the station canopy points to Glasgow Air Terminal in the row of shops beneath the stairway. The two Eastern Coach Works-bodied Bristol coaches (that on the right being an MW6G) belong to Scottish Omnibuses and are operating to Glasgow's airport at Renfrew. The dark-blue-and-cream coach behind belongs to the British Overseas Airways Corporation (BOAC) and is on the longer service to Prestwick on the Ayrshire coast, then Scotland's transatlantic airport. The Corporation Leyland Titan PD2/24 is brand-new L126, one of 75 bodied in the Coplawhill tram workshops and one of six painted in this experimental green-over-yellow livery with no cream relief; it is operating to the conservation village of Carmunnock on a route taken over from the executors of the village's bus operator, Stephen Young, in June 1941 and operated to Carlton Place until May 1957. Two Western SMT double-deckers are just visible behind L126 and the BOAC coach, on the North Drive ramp. The ornate little St Enoch station, on the left, doubled as the offices of the Glasgow District Subway from its opening in 1896 until Glasgow Corporation acquired this narrow-gauge underground railway in 1923. The cable-hauled Subway was electrified in 1935 and underwent a massive modernisation in the years 1977-80: new entrances with escalators were built at St Enoch, and the 'wee castle' became a public transport information centre. And who was St Enoch? The name is a corruption of St Thenew, mother of Glasgow's patron saint and founder, St Mungo (otherwise known as St Kentigern). *Jim Thomson*

Emerging from under the Central Station railway bridge over the Broomielaw on a 1963 morning is Newmains-bound Central SMT L420, one of 100 lowbridge all-Leyland Titan PD2/1 double-deckers new in 1948. It is in a brighter version of Central livery introduced in the mid-1950s. Glasgow Corporation also used this 'under the arches' stretch of the Broomielaw as a terminus for routes to south-side suburbs from 1946 and moved them one block north, to the even less hospitable Midland Street, in November 1963, when a new one-way traffic system affected many city-centre streets. That measure was one of the alleged traffic-management bonuses to follow the withdrawal of the last trams 14 months earlier. *Campbell Sayers*

Left: Glasgow Bridge on 9 November 1963, eight days before it became a southbound-only thoroughfare. The present road bridge opened in 1891; the original dated from 1772 and was replaced in 1836. The railway bridge behind carries trains in and out of Glasgow Central station. This nearest section of railway bridge was built when Central opened in August 1879; it was rendered redundant following resignalling in 1961 and demolished some years later, although its piers remain today. Corporation AEC Regent IIIs A225 (still with painted-over rear destination box) and A170 head north. The Regents, with Weymann bodywork to Metro-Cammell design, were from a batch of 100 new in 1951. The Godfrey Davis car-rental site on the far side of the bridge later became the jetty for today's riverbus trips to the Braehead shopping centre near Renfrew. It's also where Michael Jardine, lead character in television's *Taggart* for several years, met his end. Such is dramatic licence, though, for the scriptwriters had the police inspector's body washed ashore at Langbank, 15 miles downstream.
Iain MacGregor

Left: The Glasgow Bridge/Broomielaw junction in 1956, with 'Coronation' tram 1242 of 1939 on service 24 from Anniesland to Langside. Paisley's outfitters, sandwiched between the Central station and Jamaica Street on the Broomielaw corner, provided generations of Glaswegians with school and military uniforms. Its site — and that of the adjacent 30-department Coloseum Warehouse — remained empty for many years after it closed, but a 321-room Jury's (Scotland's largest hotel) opened there in August 2003.
The 'Coronation' is still largely in the condition in which these trams were built, with half-drop front upper-deck window and a visor above the driver's windscreen. Two 'Standard' trams — backbone of the Glasgow system — follow on services 31 and 25. The cast-metal bollard in the foreground is of a type found in few places other than Glasgow.
Frank Hunt collection / LRTA London Area

Jamaica Street was laid out in 1767 and honours one of the city's sources of international trade. This late-1950s scene shows a southbound 'Coronation' tram on service 3 from the University to Mosspark, a northbound 'Cunarder' and, just beyond it, a Weymann-bodied Daimler CVG6 bus of 1955. The visor once fitted to the 'Coronation' has been replaced with plain panelling. Both trams' upper-deck windows have had their original half-drop windows replaced by fixed glazing with a top opening, enabling conductors to reach the rope connected to the bow collector on the roof (which connects to the electricity supply) when changing direction at a terminus. In 1965 the Lions furniture and carpet shop was replaced by the Royal Stuart Hotel, which today is the Euro Hostel. The site of the huge Clydesdale furniture and television store has been empty for several years and in 2003 was being used as a temporary car park. The grey building beyond the bus is the original frontage of Boots the Chemist's main Glasgow store. Blue British Railways signs on lamp-posts either side of the street direct passengers to BR-owned Caledonian Steam Packet Co's Clyde river steamers at Bridge Wharf, next to King George V Bridge. Just visible emerging from Howard Street, below the Clydesdale building, is an all-Leyland Royal Tiger coach, probably from the Ribble fleet, which ran regularly to Glasgow from Blackpool, Morecambe, Liverpool and Manchester. *Jim Thomson*

19

This is the western end of the Hielanman's Umbrella, the bridge supporting the full width of Central station over Argyle Street, and the buffers of Platforms 12 and 13 are somewhere to the left of the Schweppes advertisement. This side of the station was added when it was virtually doubled in size between 1901 and 1906. The Umbrella earned its nickname because Highlanders who migrated to Glasgow from the mid-19th century (and worshipped nearby) are reputed to have sheltered here on the city's many wet days to converse with one another in their native Gaelic. Hope Street runs left to the north. Tram 1313 is a

'Cunarder' new in 1949 and operated until the system closed in September 1962. Although known universally as 'Cunarders' — reflecting the luxury of Clyde-built Cunard liners of the age — these hundred 70-seat bogie trams were officially 'Coronation Mk IIs'. Besides the poster next to the left-hand traffic light, publicising ferry crossings to Ireland, an advertisement over the adjacent back entrance to the station urges Glaswegians to book for travel on the new 'Blue Trains' providing south-side suburban services from May 1962.
Jim Copland / Photobus

Right: This is near the top end of Hope Street, just south of its junction with Sauchiehall Street, in 1956. Tram 1025, one of 46 1936/7 streamlined bogie trams bought from Liverpool Corporation in 1953/4, is on a short working of service 29 from Maryhill to Glasgow Cross via Normal School, short for the Normal School for the Training of Teachers at Dundas Vale. The 78-seat Liverpool cars were known in Glasgow as 'Green Goddesses', although Liverpudlians gave this name — from a George Arliss film — to an earlier generation of their city's green trams. Hope Street became one-way northbound in 1963. The white building behind has since been replaced by a brick-built structure styled sympathetically with its surroundings; the red stone building behind it is Hope Street Post Office. The shoe shop beside the tram was selling discounted books in 2003, while the unit nearer the camera had become an off-licence.
Frank Hunt collection / LRTA London Area

Below right: We're now just around the corner looking west along Sauchiehall Street — arguably the most famous of all Glasgow's streets — at its junction with Hope Street in July 1955. The name is a corruption of Sauchiehaugh and means 'meadow of willows' — a name immortalised by the Willow Tearooms, designed by Charles Rennie Mackintosh. The two four-wheel 'Standard' trams are operating circular service 33, which ran from November 1944 to May 1959; it linked this spot with Maryhill, Springburn and Townhead and was withdrawn without replacement. The Gaumont cinema began life in 1910 as The Picture House and, after several rebuilds and a change of ownership, was renamed in 1947. From April 1965 to December 1967 it screened just one film — the astonishingly popular *The Sound of Music* — but closed in 1972 to make way for the Savoy Centre indoor market. The white building behind tram 251 is Marks & Spencer's, which replaced Cranston's Waverley Hotel in 1935; Drages ('The Home of Mr & Mrs Everyone') retained its glass tiled frontage in 2003 but had become a River Island fashion shop. This section of Sauchiehall Street became one-way eastbound in 1963 before being pedestrianised in December 1973. Tram 251, with hexagonal front dash, was new in 1912 with open balconies upstairs and was scrapped in 1957. Round-dash 476 was older and lasted longer, having begun life with open top and driver's cab in 1903, and wasn't scrapped until 1959. *C. Banks collection / Colour-Rail*

Back again at the eastern side of the Umbrella in March 1962, we're looking north up Union Street at its junction with Argyle Street. It's still a two-way street and, although regular trams were withdrawn from here in June 1960, their rails remain in place. The Boots building was heavily rebuilt in 1960, has since been rebuilt again and now houses a Waterstone's bookshop. The red estate agent's hoarding in the background is on the Egyptian Halls of 1871-3 — one of the masterpieces of Glasgow's most noted early Victorian architect, Alexander 'Greek' Thomson, who drew inspiration from books of classical architecture yet never ventured abroad. Union Street breaks with the grid pattern of most city-centre streets, running at an angle between Renfield Street and Jamaica Street as it follows an old alignment of the lost village of Grahamston, which was swept away to accommodate the Central station. A bar called Grahamston's opened in the Central Hotel in 2003. Although 747 EUS, the Albion Lowlander bus in the foreground, is in Corporation livery, it is a manufacturer's demonstrator operated in the city from February 1962 to February 1963. It was built by Albion Motors in Scotstoun with Alexander bodywork from Falkirk. Route 38A was a variation of the service that replaced tram service 8, while the 44 — operated by AEC Regent III A176 — replaced tram 24 in March 1958. *Iain MacGregor*

Right: Two-way traffic on Renfield Street at its junction with West Regent Street in May 1951. These were the last years of Glasgow's route-coloured trams, and red Standard 300, new in 1909 and destined to survive until 1960, is seen heading southbound for Carnwadric on service 25. By the early 1950s 'bus' green (as on the nearly new 'Cunarder' behind) had ousted red, yellow or blue route colours from all but a few trams; white and dark green vanished by the end of World War 2. Before service numbers were introduced, in 1938, routes were organised so that, although there were three of each colour, they avoided or crossed one another rather than run in the same direction on key streets. The system pre-dated Corporation operation of the trams (from 1894) and helped at a time when there was a lower level of literacy. The timber-panelled shooting brake reminds us that parking was permitted then on city-centre streets. Fifty-two years later, the Prudential Assurance office on the left, built in 1890, is a seafood restaurant where customers may marvel at the lavish, oriental-style ceramic tiling, while the small shops beyond sell jewellery and take-away coffee. The gap to the left of tram 300 is Bath Lane, providing goods access and fire exits to these properties. *W. J. Wyse collection / LRTA London Area*

Right: Cowcaddens, at the top of Renfield Street, in September 1970. Corporation Daimler CVG6 D186 — one of 100 similar Alexander-bodied buses delivered in 1957/8 — is setting out from Maitland Street to Muirend on service 67, which replaced trolleybus 107 in March 1967. These tenements and typical corner shops (whose rental income and commercial rates helped fund Glasgow's Victorian house building boom) were soon swept away. The new Cowcaddens Road is a dual carriageway with high-rise housing to its north side. You would be forgiven for imagining that the name Cowcaddens is agricultural, but Glasgow author Carol Foreman says it was spelt Kowkaldens in the 16th century (when cattle were known as 'kye' in Scots dialect) and that this future street name translates as 'home of the unkind (or repellent) goblins'. *Brian Deans*

Left: LA1, the Corporation's first rear-engined Leyland Atlantean, passes the Transport Department's offices at 46 Bath Street, on the corner of Renfield Street and west of West Nile Street. Built originally as a four-storey structure with what are said to have been the city's first open-plan offices, 46 Bath Street had two additional storeys and a back extension added before World War 1 to accommodate the large clerical staff needed in the pre-computer age. Strathclyde PTE vacated the building in June 1982, when its staff moved to Consort House (next to Queen Street station) and the ground floor became a Garfunkels (now Filling Station) restaurant. LA1 was among the first Atlanteans built, in 1958, and was the first with an Alexander body, but (contrary to what you may read about it in the city's excellent transport museum, where it now resides), one in Wales and another in Wallasey entered service a few days earlier. It was the only Corporation Atlantean to operate in this livery and was the only one supplied without a route-number screen on the side. Clearly, someone assumed that the door was too near the front for that to be necessary, even if those approaching it from the rear were left with no clue of which route it was operating. It spent its early years operating from Ibrox garage. Service 4 linked the council estates of Balornock in the north and Drumoyne in the southwest from September 1928. A Roberts-bodied Albion Venturer is following on service 10A to Scotstounhill. *Jim Thomson*

Below left: Another May 1951 view from the top deck of a northbound tram, this time of West Nile Street just above St Vincent Street. 'Standard' tram 223 (new 1912) is on former 'red car' service 11 from Milngavie (pronounced 'Millguy') to Sinclair Drive — a route withdrawn less than two months later. Trams were withdrawn altogether from West Nile Street in July 1953, when trolleybus service 105 started. A crowd of well-dressed bystanders is watching a parade with banners in West George Street. The entrance to the Odeon cinema beyond them is in Renfield Street. Opened in December 1934 as the Paramount, this was the first purpose-built cinema in the city centre, and it is some measure of Glasgow's prewar love affair with cinema that its 2,784 seats made it the most visited Paramount outside America. Odeon bought it in 1939, and although the main Odeon today is a multi-screen complex at Springfield Quay — and the multi-storey, 18-screen UGC cinema complex at the top of West Nile Street now dominates the skyline behind — the Renfield Street Odeon was reprieved from threatened closure in 2003. Half a century later, the marble-fronted Delta House office block occupies the gap site. D. M. Hoey outfitters' shop on the right was replaced in 1968 by Scottish Life House, one of Greater Glasgow (later Strathclyde) PTE's offices from 1973 to 1982. Tracks like those to the left of the tramlines helped horse-drawn vehicles climb the cobbled streets. *W. J. Wyse collection / LRTA London Area*

The top end of West Nile Street, seen towards the end of the trolleybus era. BUT double-decker TB78 is approaching the junction where service 105 turns left into Cowcaddens to head for its northern terminus at Queen's Cross (next to Partick Thistle's Firhill football ground) and the 107 continues into Port Dundas Road to reach its terminus at nearby Maitland Street. A Holiday Inn hotel and La Bonne Auberge restaurant have replaced the tenements in recent years. The new office block under construction is Buchanan House, British Rail's Scottish headquarters, built on the carriage sidings of Buchanan Street railway station and opened in December 1967, 13 months after train services were transferred into Queen Street. The railway station entrance is the low-rise building in front of Buchanan House. TB78, delivered in 1958, was among 13 of these 90 Crossley-bodied BUTs painted in the Corporation's simplified green-over-yellow livery, which first appeared in 1959. From October to December 1964 it had the distinction of being the only trolleybus painted in the experimental 'upside down' livery shown on page 57. It is also the only surviving Glasgow double-deck trolley, preserved and operated at the Trolleybus Museum at Sandtoft, near Doncaster. *Campbell Sayers*

Above: At the top end of Buchanan Street, opposite Buchanan Street railway station (formerly the LMS main-line terminal for north and east Scotland), a line of Alexander (Midland) all-Leyland Titan TD5 and TD7 lowbridge double-deckers waits to take up duties on routes to Drumchapel, Bearsden and Milngavie. This is August 1961, three months after the Alexander fleet — with almost 2,000 buses in west, central and northeast Scotland — was split in three. The Midland company retained Alexander's distinctive blue livery and 967 buses. Remarkably, all five of these buses are of prewar design. R230 was one of 28 TD5s delivered in 1939. The 105 route, to the huge mid-1950s Glasgow Corporation housing scheme at Drumchapel, was one of several routes kept out of the congested bus station by terminating instead in nearby Renfrew Street, a stance area designated in the 1920s. *Brian Patton*

Right: In his comprehensive 1946 history of Glasgow, *The Second City*, Charles Oakley commented that the otherwise handsome Buchanan Street (named after 18th-century tobacco merchant Andrew Buchanan) lost its distinction north of West George Street and lacked something architecturally worthwhile at its north end. Were he still alive today, he might well be pleased that this finest of all the

city's shopping streets has been pedestrianised, with the imposing Royal Concert Hall and Buchanan Galleries shopping mall added at the north. In this May 1970 view looking south, Corporation Atlantean LA92 and three forward-entrance AEC Regent Vs are milling around near where escalator entrances to Buchanan Street Subway station can be found today. The Regents are bound for Drumchapel and Knightswood in the west, while LA92 is at the city terminus of an eastbound express service to Easterhouse, which started a month earlier. The orange dot on its front roof dome was a feature of the Corporation's first one-man-operated double-deckers. The styling of Alexander's bodywork leapt forward in the four years between the arrival of LA1 and LA2. There was no LA91, incidentally, as Leyland bought it back from the Corporation in March 1963 and demonstrated it to other bus operators for the next two years. The Ivanhoe (previously Waverley) Hotel has become the Buchanan Hotel, while the former Athenaeum Theatre and Royal Scottish Academy of Music next door were vacant in 2003. The steeple is that of St George's Tron church, built in 1807 in what used to be St George's Place and is now Nelson Mandela Place. *Iain MacGregor*

Within yards of the previous picture, we're entering the part of the city centre most drastically altered over the past 20 years. The photographer is standing at the junction of Buchanan Street and Cathedral Street, looking northeast as Leyland Titan PD2/24 L103 (with Alexander-designed body assembled in the Corporation's Coplawhill tramcar works) makes its way west into Bath Street *en route* from South Carntyne to Scotstounhill. The Five Ways Lounge bar, the Buchanan Hotel and the tenements have long gone and the Buchanan Galleries spans this junction, with a Sainsbury's convenience store where the black Ford saloon is passing the pub. Beyond the tenements is the site of an already demolished church on the corner of Dundas Street and the fencing visible above the grey Ford Thames lorry marks the edge of Queen Street station, whose platforms lie deep below. *Roy Marshall / Photobus*

Right: Buchanan Street ends today at the steps leading into the Royal Concert Hall, which opened in 1990. The lost section north of there included Buchanan Street bus station, opened by the Scottish Motor Traction group in 1934 for services that until then had used stances in Cathedral Street. It was used mainly by Alexander, SMT and Central SMT buses, but Western SMT also used it for its first couple of years for routes to Kilmarnock, Ayr and beyond. The adjacent Massey's greengrocer's shop had been demolished by February 1975, when Alexander (Midland) MT20, a Ford R1114 with Alexander Y-type body, was recorded emerging into Buchanan Street using what, for most of the bus station's life, was its exit. This was originally the entrance, and the design envisaged buses leaving by the individual platform doorways on the northern and eastern sides of the building in Germiston Street and Killermont Street; probably because of this original design, Central SMT continued to describe it as Killermont Street bus station. The bus station closed in 1976, and the site is buried somewhere beneath today's Killermont Street, which runs roughly east–west and is substantially longer than the original, which ran from south to north. *Alan Millar*

Right: About the only navigational aid for anyone visiting this part of town today is Lang's Hotel, next to the 1976 Buchanan bus station and built on the site of the former British Railways office building at 302 Buchanan Street. It's the block behind Scottish Omnibuses Leyland Titan PD1 HH21, seen turning out of Germiston Street in 1964, with the corner of the bus station next to the Reid's bakers' BMC J2 van. The BR office later became a Scottish Bus Group travel centre and parcel office. HH21 was new to Central SMT in February 1947, transferred to Scottish Omnibuses 15 years later and remained until 1966. The paper bills in the downstairs front window show it is running to Chapelhall via Lightburn, one of the housing estates off the Edinburgh Road. *Campbell Sayers*

Below: Alexander's relieved congestion at the Buchanan Street site in 1944 by building Dundas Street bus station, an open-air terminal close by on the south-eastern corner of the Dundas Street/Killermont Street and Parliamentary Road crossroads. Both bus stations were next door to the warehouses of Buchanan Street goods station, Glasgow's busiest pre-World War 1 rail freight terminal. This 1960 photograph shows RD16, a 1956 Bristol Lodekka LD6G of the David Lawson fleet, turning into the bus station from Parliamentary Road, with its destination blind already set for the return journey to Auchinairn. It's about to pass one of Alexander's Duple-bodied Guy Arab III single-deckers, as a passer-by studies the long list of day and half-day tours then on offer. Kirkintilloch-based Lawson's started trading in 1923 and was acquired by Alexander's in 1936 but retained its identity and SMT-group red livery until 1961, when it was wound up on creation of the new Midland company. The Scottish Bus Group renamed it Clydeside Omnibuses and kept that name alive until 1978, initially with a view to splitting Western SMT in two, later in hopes of using it to take over Glasgow Corporation Transport. The buildings behind, including the Parly Road Café and George Boyd builders' merchants, were demolished long before the bus station closed in 1976. Don't let anyone tell you that the false sash windows above the café were anything to do with window tax. That was abolished long before Glasgow's Victorian tenements were built; this was an architect's trick to balance the appearance of buildings where no glazing was needed. *Ian Stewart*

Right: Fast forward to Parliamentary Road on a summer's morning in 1976, and the 177 from Dundas Street to Auchinairn is Alexander (Midland) MRF123, a rear-engined Daimler Fleetline with low-height Alexander body. Its advertisement for Murphy televisions speaks volumes of the poor reliability of early colour sets. The red brick wall to its right is the Killermont Street side of Buchanan Street bus station; beyond that, 302 Buchanan Street has become the Scottish Bus Group travel centre, and the site of the Parly Road Café has long since become an overspill bus-parking area. Crowds of luggage-laden long-distance passengers are milling around what passed for coaches that day; the poppy-red-and-turquoise (officially 'peacock blue') single-decker is a Highland Omnibuses Ford. The new Buchanan bus station — off-camera to the right — opened before Christmas that year. Behind is a PTE Metropolitan double-decker on the short-lived Centre Circle service. *Stuart Little*

Left: An evening scene at Dundas Street bus station in the mid-1960s, as immaculately uniformed employees, passengers, friends and families gather around two Western SMT Leyland Leopards preparing to leave on the overnight service to London. These were among the most luxuriously equipped coaches in Britain at the time, with generous legroom and on-board toilets (even tartan blankets in winter). Both vehicles have Alexander bodywork; the nearer is a 38-seat Y-type dating from 1963 or 1964, the other a 30-seater new in 1960. The Forfarshire Bar is on the corner of Killermont Street and Parliamentary Road. The Royal Concert Hall now occupies the bus-station site, and Parliamentary Road — stretching from the eastern end of Sauchiehall Street to Castle Street at Townhead — has been erased from the map, although today's Killermont Street is built over part of it.
Robert Grieves

In another effort to relieve congestion at Buchanan Street bus station, Scottish Omnibuses — the renamed original SMT company, which later called itself Eastern Scottish — for a time used Cunningham Street as the terminus of its route to/from Easterhouse, another of Glasgow's huge 1950s council estates. This long-vanished side street (Holmhead Street until renamed in 1922 to avoid confusion with Holmhead Road in Cathcart, on the south side) was over the wall from Dundas Street bus station and perched on a bridge high above Queen Street railway station. This is 1964, and Bristol Lodekka FLF6G AA873C is parked ahead of an LD-type Lodekka. The modern office block is 15-storey St Andrew House, opened that year on the corner of Sauchiehall Street and West Nile Street. *Campbell Sayers*

Left: The comprehensively redeveloped Townhead area is built over the lengthy eastern portion of Parliamentary Road. Tin baths were still in demand from the hardware shop behind Corporation Daimler CWA6 DR9 as it entered Parliamentary Road from Monkland Street on tram replacement service 38 from Millerston to Rouken Glen — a large country park donated to the city in 1906 by Lord Rowallan and which became a popular leisure destination for tram passengers. The 38 bus replaced the 8 tram in March 1959. When delivered in 1944, DR9 was numbered 116 and had an austere wartime utility body built by Northern Counties of Wigan. One of 30 similar 1943-6 Daimlers rebodied in 1954 by East Lancashire Coachbuilders, it was scrapped in 1963.
Jim Thomson

Below: David MacBrayne's coach services to various West Coast destinations operated out of a rudimentary garage-cum-coach station at the Townhead end of Parliamentary Road. This long-established bus, shipping and haulage company was part-owned from 1928 by the LMS railway and later by the state. It became part of the new state-owned Scottish Transport Group in 1969, and most of its bus services transferred to Scottish Bus Group subsidiaries the following year. This is the final departure of its last mainland service — to Campbeltown via Inveraray, Ardrishaig and Tarbert — on 3 October 1970. Willowbrook-bodied AEC Reliance No 170, turning out of the station into Hartfield Street, joined the Highland Omnibuses fleet, but Western SMT took over this route the next afternoon using its own black-and-white Leyland Leopards. Parliamentary Road coach station closed the following February, when SBG moved into its new Anderston bus station. The MacBrayne name and clansman logo survive as part of Caledonian MacBrayne, a still-state-owned ferry company. The vertical advertisement on the wall next to the coach is for India tyres, whose art-deco factory was at Inchinnan, near Renfrew.
Ian Maclean

Glasgow's first bus station, in Waterloo Street, opened c1927 as a combined garage and terminus for the Glasgow General Omnibus Co, one of the constituent parts of Central SMT. It was built on a vacant plot of land just west of Hope Street, at the junction with Wellington Street, where the Caledonian Railway had bought a site for the then yet-to-be-built Central station. Central SMT (formed in 1932) made most use of Waterloo Street, but there were a few Scottish Omnibuses departures, and Western SMT transferred its Ayr Road routes from the congested Buchanan Street bus station to Waterloo Street in 1937. In this 1966 view, passengers for Central's Lanarkshire services are queuing into Waterloo Street itself, while L340, a Leyland Titan PD2/1 of 1951, prepares to leave on Central's frequent service to Balloch, at the south end of Loch Lomond. A Western SMT Daimler Fleetline is at the platform beyond. The Waterloo Street terminal suffered from the problem that led to Buchanan Street bus station's being turned back-to-front; buses entered from a side entrance in Wellington Street and often queued into the street when waiting for a vacant platform. After it closed in February 1971, a Civil Service office block was built on the site; this has since been demolished, however, and a new commercial development — Central Exchange — was due to open there in 2004. *Robert Grieves*

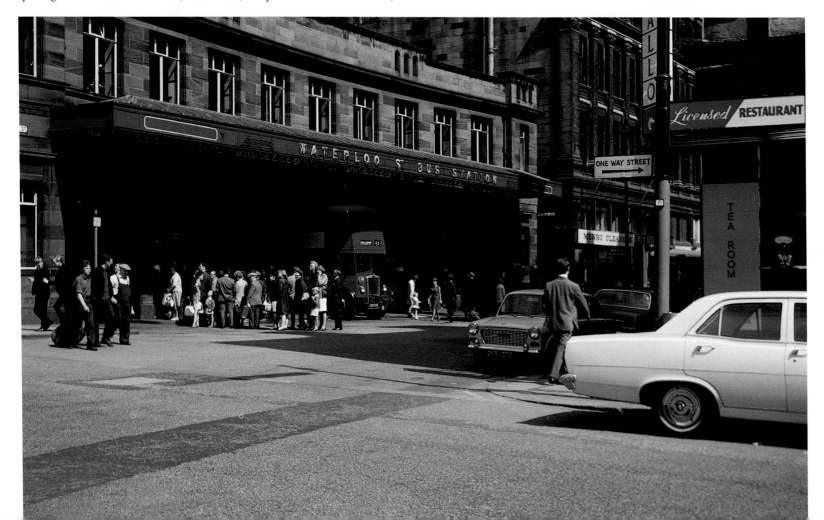

Right: This is farther down Wellington Street in late 1959 or early 1960, near the junction with Argyle Street. Waterloo Street bus station is the low-rise building three blocks behind. The bus is 80 WMH, a Park Royal-bodied AEC Bridgemaster demonstrator, on Central SMT's Glasgow–Newmains service. The standard Central destination blind is too shallow for the space allowed by Park Royal, so, as well as 'Newmains', it is showing the top couple of inches of 'New Stevenston', which is on a different route. By this time Central was buying Leylands and Bristols and thus didn't order any low-height Bridgemasters — but then neither did many other operators. In 1960 an Essex operator bought 80 WMH, which would be rebuilt in later life as a mock vintage bus to appeal to London tourists. *Jim Thomson*

Below right : Corporation Leyland Titan PD3A/2 L398 in Argyle Street — west of the city centre — in 1966, at the site on the corner of Blythswood Street where the Scottish Bus Group's Anderston bus station opened in February 1971. This new facility — part of a large office development — replaced Waterloo Street and Parliamentary Road bus stations as well as the Clyde Street and St Enoch Square stances but was less centrally located and offered few comforts for waiting passengers. It closed in 1993. Alexander-bodied L398 was a unique vehicle in the Corporation fleet and was exhibited at the Commercial Motor Show in London in September 1960. Although broadly similar to 139 PD3s delivered 1960-2, it was the only one with this style of glassfibre bonnet and also had a much brighter interior, with fluorescent (rather than tungsten) lighting and mainly cream (rather than green) panelling. It was among the first buses in the fleet with enclosed forward (rather than open rear) entrances — a safety measure that anticipated the four-lane one-way traffic system introduced in 1963. If you worry about such things, the registration number (SGD 400) — like that of many contemporary Glasgow Leylands — was two adrift of its fleetnumber. The Corporation Transport Department reserved all the FYS and SGD registration series for its own use. *Robert Grieves*

Hardly anything remains of Anderston as it existed on 10 March 1962, the day before bus 62 replaced tram 15 to Baillieston. Indeed, so drastic was the redevelopment of the area (its population falling from 31,902 in 1951 to 9,265 in 1971) that Argyle Street, which ran continuously from Trongate to Dumbarton Road, has been broken in three. Today the eastern section continues straight into Stobcross Street (whence the Austin A55 Cambridge is emerging) to join the Clydeside Expressway past the old Queen's Dock. The section in the left foreground (where children are playing next to a Guinness lorry) is isolated and virtually traffic-free, while the busier western section resumes west of St Vincent Street. The City Pawnbroking Co is on the corner of Washington Street, and the Kingston Bridge (opened June 1970) now carries the M8 high above this site, with Anderston low-level railway station directly behind the photographer. As early as May 1967, redevelopment cut the 62 back to Wellington Street, near where the Bridgemaster demonstrator is seen on page 37. The tram about to terminate at Anderston Cross is 'Coronation' 1144, new in November 1937 and withdrawn a week before the system closed in September 1962. *Iain MacGregor*

The Kingston Bridge, associated motorway construction and massive office developments also greatly altered Bothwell Street. Alexander 'Greek' Thomson's St Vincent Street United Presbyterian Church of 1859 is all that remains from this scene one quiet Sunday in September 1964, when the modest hair stylist's, tobacconist's and lunchroom were all closed for the day. The George & Jobling car showroom made way for Heron House, a high-rise office block used in its time by the British National Oil Corporation (later called Britoil) and Abbey National. It's a sign of how Glasgow is changing that it has been converted to The Pinnacle, a 21st-century apartment complex. Bothwell Street followed the alignment of the diagonal building behind the showroom before the Kingston Bridge slip roads were built. The bus is Central SMT L446, a 1951 Leyland Titan PD1A with Northern Counties body, on the last stage of its journey from Balloch to Waterloo Street. Lanarkshire registration PVD 700 on the Ford Consul would be worth a small fortune today. *Iain MacGregor*

Left: The former Beresford Hotel at the Charing Cross end of Sauchiehall Street, built in 1938 to house visitors to that year's Empire Exhibition at Bellahouston Park, is Glasgow's most noted art-deco building. It took its name from its managing director, former cinema owner William Beresford Inglis, but it wasn't a success. Postwar it was converted first into offices for ICI, later becoming Strathclyde University's Baird Hall of Residence, but as this is being written it is on the market again, likely to join the many city-centre buildings converted into apartments. Since this picture was taken in Elmbank Street *c*1965, it has regained something closer to its original yellow façade. The building behind Corporation Atlantean LA226 is Lyon's stationery shop, which closed after a dramatic fatal accident in the mid-1960s when a runaway lorry rolled down Garnet Street beside the Beresford and embedded itself in the shop. The graffiti

behind the car is the Scottish National Party logo, reflecting one direction of political thinking at the time. This was as close as bus 32, which replaced tram 16, got to the city centre on its way from Keppochhill Road to Scotstoun. *Ian Stewart*

Above: Charing Cross was also greatly changed by motorway construction. This is St George's Road at the Woodlands Road junction. While the St George's Mansions flats and most of the buildings on the left survive, everything on the right has gone, and the M8 thunders in their place in a cutting below. The street climbing off to the right of Atlantean LA140 (commandeered temporarily for driver tuition) is aptly named Hill Street, now truncated in Garnethill, on the opposite side of the motorway. *Ian Stewart*

Left: The Kelvin Hall, opened in 1927 to replace an earlier structure burnt down in 1925, was Scotland's principal venue for exhibitions before the Scottish Exhibition & Conference Centre replaced it in 1985. It also contained an arena for sports events and concerts. Several new Glasgow Corporation buses (and a few painted to look as if they were) made their debuts at the two-yearly Scottish Motor Show held here until 1938 and again from 1949 to 1983. It also played host to Modern Homes Exhibitions, to an annual carnival and circus and to such special events as rallies by the American evangelist Billy Graham. It reopened in 1985 when the Museum of Transport (in which seven Corporation trams, two buses and a trolleybus take pride of place) moved here from the former Coplawhill tram works in Pollokshields. The museum hopes to move again to a purpose-built riverside site in 2009, and there is talk of retaining the Kelvin Hall façade and selling the rest of the site for housing. In this April 1960 view, with part of the Western Infirmary in the background, 'Cunarder' tram 1299 of 1949 heads from Scotstoun to Mosshouse, a long-forgotten intermediate destination in north Glasgow. The bus just visible on the right is one of 15 1937 AEC Regents rebodied by Alexander in 1950 and withdrawn later in 1960.
Colour-Rail

Above: The Kelvingrove Art Gallery & Museum, built for the 1901 International Exhibition, when Glasgow demonstrated its wealth to the rest of the Empire, is across Dumbarton Road from the Kelvin Hall. Although most visitors approach and enter the red sandstone building from this side, strictly speaking this is the back, as it was designed to face the River Kelvin. For decades the museum has exhibited the city's art collection (the likes of Rubens, Monet and Van Gogh, as well as numerous Scottish artists) in addition to natural history and coats of armour. It closed in 2003 for a massive refit likely to take several years. The Corporation bus is 1959 Alexander-bodied Leyland Titan PD2/24 L267 on service 32, which replaced tram 16 from Keppochhill Road to Scotstoun. It was converted into a breakdown lorry in 1970 and was sold 12 years later.
Alistair Douglas / Photobus

Great Western Road — linking St George's Cross with Anniesland Toll — was developed in the mid-19th century. This unbelievably tranquil scene, with 1922-built 'hex dash' 'Standard' tram 35 on service 1 to Dennistoun, is at Botanic Gardens in the late-1950s. The ornate building on the right is the former Botanic Gardens station on the Kirklee branch of the Central low level line, which opened in 1896. Although trains would operate through it until 1964, trams had taken away 90% of its business by 1911, and it closed in 1939. In this picture, the bright-green-fronted Silver Slipper café has moved into the western end of the building. It was still there, along with Sgt Pepper's nightclub, when the building burned down in January 1970. A Corporation AEC Regent V is following alongside the 44-acre park, which opened in 1891, as a blue Alexander's double-decker disappears in the distance. *Jim Thomson*

Right: Close to the same spot in May 1951, two-month-old AEC Regent III A166 overtakes 593, a prewar Regent new in July 1938, when Glasgow played host to the Empire Exhibition. Both have Weymann bodies built in Surrey, A166's to Metro-Cammell design, while 593's is typical of 189 AECs, Leylands, Daimlers and Albions delivered between 1937 and 1942. Two other Regent IIIs follow, while a 'Standard' tram disappears west along one of few stretches of road with tramlines laid in tarmac rather than granite setts. A166 was the first of 100 such buses new in 1951/2 and was scrapped in 1967; 593 (one of 100 Corporation buses with appropriate 'BUS' registrations) was taken out of service later in 1951 but saw further service with a Carlisle operator. Route 11, from Yoker in the west, normally extended beyond Castle Street to Provanmill in the northeast; it started in 1930 and served this section of Great Western Road from 1934 until First Glasgow diverted it through Kelvindale and Hyndland in 2002. The 3 began in 1926 as a shuttle route between nearby Kelvindale and Botanic Gardens, was extended to the city centre in 1927 and reached Mosspark in the southwest from January 1929; the Kelvindale–City Centre section was withdrawn in November 1974.
W. J. Wyse collection / LRTA London Area

Right: The same junction in September 1970, looking south rather than west, as one-man-operated Corporation Atlantean LA191 crosses Great Western Road from Byres Road towards Queen Margaret Drive. Grosvenor Terrace behind was built in 1855 and was designed by the architect J. T. Rochead, also responsible for the Wallace Monument outside Stirling. The Grosvenor Hotel, first opened in the 1930s and expanded into adjoining properties, was totally destroyed by fire in January 1978 during a national firefighters' strike. Happily, it was rebuilt with a replica façade based closely on the original design. The elegant terraces along this stretch of road were threatened with the loss of their service roads earlier in the 1970s, when highway plans envisaged widening Great Western Road to create an arterial expressway. The green Post Office Telephones (predecessor of BT) Morris Minor van fast disappearing to the right of the picture is advertising extension phones. U-shaped route 33, introduced in November 1944, was another that didn't reach the city centre; it linked Blairdardie and Gairbraid Avenue, Maryhill, with Partick and Hillhead.
Brian Deans

A mile-and-three-quarters farther west along Great Western Road, a 'Coronation' tram on service 10 turns into Hyndland Road on the last leg of its journey to Kelvinside. Cleveden Road climbs behind past mansions towards the inter-war suburb of Kelvindale, which never saw trams and got its first bus service in 1926. Is the man in the gabardine mac telling the little girl to take a last look at the tram before it passes into history? The yellow sign to the right of his head reads 'Take care — Accident area'; the red tram-stop sign below the yellow Corporation bus-stop flag reads 'Cars stop here if required'. To most Glaswegians, trams were 'cars' or 'caurs'. Bus service 43 replaced tram 5 from Kelvinside to Holmlea Road in November 1957, but the 10 to London Road survived until June 1960, when bus 59 provided a partial replacement.
Jim Thomson

In 1936 Great Western Road was widened into a dual carriageway from Hughenden, a short distance west of Kelvinside, with trams diverted onto the central median. In this scene from the late 1950s, westbound 'hex dash' 'Standard' tram 73 of 1920, on service 1 to Scotstoun West, is about to pass beneath the railway bridge on the former LNER Queen Street low-level system; Anniesland station is to the right of the bridge. The 1,900-seat Gaumont cinema — screening Cary Grant in *North by Northwest* when this picture was taken — opened in December 1939 (Scotland's last prewar cinema) as the Ascot but changed its name in 1950 and again in 1964, when it became the Odeon. After it closed in 1975, it became a bingo hall but was rebuilt again in 2003 as the Picture House, with luxury flats towering above its art-deco façade. Initial asking-prices for two-bedroom flats were around £200,000. Few of the four-wheel 'Standard' trams survived long after routes 1 and 30 were withdrawn in March 1960, as only they could easily negotiate those routes' sharp turns at Parkhead Cross, in the East End. *Jim Thomson*

By the standards of today's traffic, it's hard to believe that this picture was taken at around 08.00 on a weekday and that this was a late-1950s rush-hour scene at Anniesland Cross, a short distance west of the previous view. With most seats already filled, A45, a Crossley-bodied AEC Regent III, has turned out of Bearsden Road into Great Western Road and will turn right again into Crow Road on a short working of service 16 through the city centre to Castle Street. A 'Standard' tram is on the Great Western Road central reservation on the line towards Knightswood Cross and Blairdardie. The bus immediately to the left of A45 is almost certainly an AEC Regent V (if not, it's a Daimler CVG6) with Weymann-designed body on its way to Knightswood, a large estate of quality council houses built between the wars. Anniesland Road runs off towards the left, with two low-rise sheds of the Corporation's Knightswood bus garage (Europe's largest when opened in 1930, and based on a similar facility in Berlin); the two buses turning into Great Western Road beyond the tram are emerging from the other side of this huge depot, which First Glasgow closed in January 2004. Service 16 started in 1934, linking Knightswood with George Square; it was extended northeast to Stobhill Hospital in 1937, then to Balornock East in 1948. Recent First Glasgow route revisions take it south instead of east, to East Kilbride New Town. *Jim Thomson*

We're back on Dumbarton Road, west of the Kelvin Hall and Art Galleries, riding on the top of an eastbound tram at Partick Hill station in April 1962. A nearly new electric 'Blue Train' in Caledonian Railway kingfisher blue speeds over the bridge while 'Coronation' tram 1269, new November 1939, heads towards Scotstoun on service 26 from Dalmarnock. This was Glasgow's second-last tram route, replaced on 3 June 1962 by bus 63. Partick depot, reached down Hayburn Street by the tracks leading off to the right, closed with service 26, and tram 1269 was among the vehicles also retired that day. A powerfully atmospheric and emotional film, *9 Dalmuir West*, was filmed in black-and-white when Partick depot closed and is preserved in the Scottish Film Archive. Catch it if you can. The depot reopened as a bus garage in 1964, only to close again in 1977. The 'Blue Trains', with their logo of interlocking blue and yellow chevrons symbolising respectively the converging banks of the Clyde and the trains' pantographs, were a *quid pro quo* for Glasgow Corporation's withdrawal of most tram and bus services beyond the city boundary. The north-side services through Partick Hill and Queen Street low-level started in November 1960, only to be suspended from December 1960 to October 1961 while serious teething troubles were rectified. They served the area well, and the last of the original trains — long since repainted orange — was retired at the beginning of 2003. Partick was beyond the city boundaries until November 1912, when this burgh was absorbed into the city after 60 years' independent existence. Its independence lasted long enough for it to have powers to issue 'YS' vehicle registration marks. *Colour-Rail*

Left: Beyond Partick, Dumbarton Road reaches Scotstoun, another riverside shipbuilding and engineering community. This is Scotstoun West in 1956 as maximum-traction bogie tram 1106, built by Hurst Nelson of Motherwell in 1928, heads east on final route 9 to its wonderfully titled eastern terminus at Auchenshuggle. If ever there was an onomatopoetic name for a tram terminus, it was this one, with the third syllable pronounced 'shoogle' — also a Scots dialect word that perfectly expresses the shake, rattle and roll of a speeding tram. Indeed, many Glaswegians referred affectionately to their trams as 'shooglies'. The 51 maximum-traction cars — most, unusually for Glasgow, built by three commercial contractors rather than the Corporation — were known to enthusiasts as 'Kilmarnock Bogies', as their bogies were built by the Kilmarnock Engineering Co. They spent most of their lives on these long, straight routes after city-centre derailments led to their removal from the long routes linking Paisley with Airdrie and Uddingston in Lanarkshire. The Gambols, advertised on the side of the tram, were the central characters in a long-running *Daily Express* and *Sunday Express* cartoon strip by Dobs and Barry Appleby. *Frank Hunt collection / LRTA London Area*

Left: Scotstoun West viewed westwards in 1959, with the tramlines from Kingsway and Anniesland coming in from the right. The railway bridge — still in place 44 years later as a cycle way — is a branch off the Lanarkshire & Dunbartonshire Railway, which connected into the Central low-level system and closed in 1964. The private car to the left of the trams is in Burnham Street, which leads under the main L&D railway to South Street, the Yarrow shipyard and Albion Motors, Scotland's most successful indigenous bus and truck manufacturer. At least one of the two British Road Services lorries in Kingsway is an Albion. The two 'Standard' trams approaching the camera are operating special journeys for shipyard workers (the leading one apparently bound for Possilpark), as is Partick-bound single-decker 1089, a unique inter-urban bogie tram built in 1926 to combat competition from private buses but which spent much of its life on this and other short-haul work; it is preserved in Glasgow's Museum of Transport. The other 'Standard' is on a peak-hour service 1 to Dalmuir West. The orange-and-cream bus shelter on the right is in Anniesland Road, used by bus 15 from Blairdardie. *Chris Bennett / Martin Jenkins / Online Transport Archive*

Kingsway at Scotstoun West on 13 March 1960, the day bus service 58 replaced tram service 1. Dumbarton Road is behind, with a Central SMT Leyland Titan exiting stage left towards Glasgow near where tram 1106 appears opposite. A270 is a 1955 AEC Regent V with Weymann-designed bodywork built by Alexander in Stirling. It was one of 75 such buses (50 bodied by Alexander and the other 25 by Weymann in Surrey), which were unusual in having preselector gearboxes and Gardner (rather than AEC) engines. Along with 75 similar Leylands and Daimlers, they represented a crossroads in Glasgow motorbus design: on one hand, they were the first with wide bonnets and concealed radiators; on the other, they were the last built to the old 7ft 6in (rather than the new 8ft) width limit and with varnished wood (rather than painted metal) interiors. A270 was one of relatively few buses supplied at the time with saloon heaters, the bulge hanging from the ceiling next to the driver's cab forming part of the equipment. This luxury — at a time when heaters were still 'optional extras' on private cars — was provided mainly for buses used on all-night services. *Jim Thomson*

Left: The western terminus of route 9 was at Dalmuir West, beyond the city boundary and almost at the far end of the adjoining burgh of Clydebank — a burgh so independent that it staged its own last tram run on 6 September 1962, two days after the main event in Glasgow. The final stage of the journey took trams over the 1915 Forth & Clyde Canal swing bridge, in the direction that Central SMT L608 is taking here. From 1908 to 1928 the Dumbarton Burgh & County Tramways Co provided a connecting service from Dalmuir to Balloch. Here, a Belisha beacon appears to be bowing in reverence as slightly dented 'Cunarder' 1362 of 1950 heads back into Clydebank and Balloch- or Helensburgh-bound L608, an Alexander-bodied Leyland Titan PD2/30 of 1959, crosses the canal towards its home depot at Old Kilpatrick. The blue British Railways sign behind the Belisha beacon points to Dalmuir Riverside station on the Lanarkshire & Dunbartonshire line, while the sign under the Co-op advertisement points towards the Arnott Young scrapyard at Dalmuir, where many redundant trams were reduced to their component metal parts. *Jim Thomson*

Below: Another view of the swing bridge, from the canal bank in August 1962, as a less-than-pristine 'Coronation' crosses, with Dalmuir Park rising on the left. The canal closed on 1 January 1963 but reopened in 2002 in a millennium project that allows boat owners to take their pleasure craft from Bowling, west of here, to Edinburgh via the Forth & Clyde and Union canals. *A. P. Tatt*

The Forth & Clyde Canal route east from Dalmuir takes it through Maryhill, an independent burgh absorbed by Glasgow in 1891. Although this is a city of many more than Rome's seven hills (and the word 'hill' figures in the names of a good few of its districts), Maryhill, in the northwest of the city, is named after a person. One Mary Hill inherited the Gairbraid Estate and agreed that the canal be built there in the 1770s on condition that the new village took her name. This 29 April 1960 scene shows tram 1036 — by then one of the last three ex-Liverpool 'Green Goddesses' and the last of all when withdrawn that July — heading along Maryhill Road towards the city on service 29 to Calderpark Zoo, beyond Glasgow's eastern boundary at Broomhouse. The right-hand destination box reads 'Zoo'. The Tollcross–Broomhouse section of the 29 closed in November 1960, the rest of the route became bus 61 in October 1961, and the zoo closed in August 2003. Until February 1954 Maryhill terminus was in

Caldercuilt Road, the side street next to the Alexander's Burlingham Seagull coach behind the tram, but it was moved to Maryhill Park (near the 'Coronation' tram in the distance) to accommodate the bulkier Liverpool trams. The Alexander's bus in the foreground is AC64 — a 1955 AEC Monocoach with Alexander bodywork — from the company's Balfron garage; it is operating one of the routes into the Campsie Hills beyond Milngavie. Maryhill Park station, to the left of the 'Goddess', is on the former North British line from Queen Street. It closed in October 1961, but suburban services were restored in the 1990s. Before railway nationalisation, this station was plain and simple Maryhill, but it was renamed to avoid confusion with the former Caledonian Maryhill (renamed Maryhill Central). Maryhill tram depot is behind the photographer, on the opposite side of the road. *Colour-Rail*

Maryhill also was home to one of the secrets of the Corporation bus network, single-deck service 24. This ran between Gairbraid Avenue (opposite Maryhill Library) and nearby Gilshochill and was extended farther up the hill to Cadder (pronounced 'Cawdor') in 1954. Its original route took it under a low canal aqueduct in Lochburn Road, but it was diverted away from there in 1959. The route was so short that drivers and conductors seldom bothered to change the destination blinds. Here, LS22 — a 1957 Leyland Royal Tiger Worldmaster — descends Sandbank Street past a 'deaf children' sign, one of Glasgow's many 'Tardis' police boxes and a typical Corporation bus shelter close to Maryhill Road. This was shortly before one-man-operated Panther single-deckers replaced the conductor-and-driver Worldmasters in July 1970; such was the unreliability of the replacement buses that double-deckers took over in 1975, and a mainstream service was later extended over its route. The Worldmasters on the 24 were the last of 30 delivered 1956-8. Their Weymann bodies were fitted out in the Corporation's Coplawhill tramcar works with 40 seats and two doors, with a view to converting quieter routes to one-man operation; that didn't happen, and all were rebuilt 1960-3 with 44 seats and one door. Twelve were sold as early as 1965. *Brian Deans*

Left: Substantial aqueducts help carry the canal through Maryhill. This is the replacement structure built over Bilsland Drive, just off Maryhill Road, in 1879. In this 22 May 1961 view, 'Coronation' tram 1195 (new 1938) is about to pass under it on its way from Springburn to Shawfield on service 18A, a variation of the 18 to Burnside in the southeast. Less than a fortnight later, on 4 June, bus services 18 and 18A took over — the only time a cross-city tram service was replaced by buses using the same route numbers. Forty-two years later, bus 18 still follows much of the eastern section of the tram route, but it starts in East Kilbride, and the western and northwestern sections have changed. *Colour-Rail*

Above: Permanent waving is on offer at the ladies' and gents' hairdressers on the corner of Millarbank Street and Keppochhill Road in Cowlairs (the north-Glasgow heart of the once thriving steam-locomotive industry) in November 1964. Forward-entrance AEC Regent V A426 is setting out for Scotstoun on tram-replacement service 32. This was one of 22 buses (nine Regents, eight Titan PD2s, three Atlanteans, a Daimler and a trolleybus) repainted that autumn in an 'upside-down' livery of deeper shades of green and yellow. Although the green panels should have worn better than the yellow, there was a public outcry against the change, with some passengers claiming to have missed what they didn't recognise as a Corporation bus. The experiment was duly abandoned, and all 22 buses were repainted green-over-yellow by December 1964. *Ian Maclean*

Left: In 1942 Glasgow Corporation indulged in what marketeers today would call 'rebranding', by changing the name of the northern district of Garngad to Royston; Garngadhill became Roystonhill, and Garngad Road, leading between Castle Street and Robroyston, became Royston Road. This is Darnick Street, the Royston Road terminus of trolleybus route 101, on 1 September 1962 — a Saturday when more attention and cameras were focused on the end of normal tram services a few miles away. Nevertheless, Weymann-bodied Sunbeam F4A No TG15, bound for Shawfield, is also playing its small part in the city's transport history: the following morning, after 12 years, the 101 and 102 swapped northern termini, the 101 being extended to Riddrie and the 102 cut back to Royston Road on a reduced frequency. The turning circle has brought TG15 along Forge Street from the right, past the green Cowlairs Co-operative Society Albion delivery van. *Iain MacGregor*

Below left: We've moved to the East End and Duke Street, Dennistoun, in 1959, where 50-year-old 'round dash' 'Standard' tram 288 and 47-year-old 'hex dash' 245 are passing 1949 Roberts-bodied Albion Venturer bus B52 while men in cloth caps converse over an electricity junction box. The trolleybus wires take service 106 off to the right along Cumbernauld Road towards its terminus at Millerston; those coming straight overhead lead to Dennistoun tram depot, a short distance behind the photographer. Duke Street station, on the Springburn branch of the Queen Street low-level system, is even closer behind him. Dennistoun depot housed 18 trolleybuses from June 1958 until it closed in November 1960. Forty-four years later the buildings in the picture were still standing, but the National Bank on the left had become a tanning salon, the hairdresser's on the right a cosmetic denture specialist. This was one of a few places where quite separate Corporation tram and bus services ran with duplicated numbers. Tram service 1 (Scotstoun West–Dalmarnock) and bus service 1 (Killermont–Sandyhills) followed the same lengthy section of route between the eastern end of St Vincent Street and the start of Shettleston Road, yet the travelling public seemed to know the difference between the two. Bus routes were numbered from the mid-1920s, and there were services up to 26 when numbers began replacing route colours on trams in 1938. Regular tram services were numbered from 1 to 21, and wartime and subsequent changes added 27 to 36, plus 40. When the tram-replacement programme got underway in 1957 there were bus services numbered up to 51, although 43 and 44 were vacant, and the original 45 was abandoned three months before tram 25 was withdrawn. *Chris Bennett / Martin Jenkins / Online Transport Archive*

Above: Shettleston Road, which branches off Duke Street, in 1957, when the privately owned Lowland Motorways fleet included Glasgow's first two rear-engined double-deck buses. These were Leyland Lowloaders — lightweight, low-height buses with a tiny engine located under the staircase on the back platform. They were demonstration and development vehicles that helped Leyland evolve the design into the revolutionary Atlantean, with its entrance and driver's cab ahead of the front axle. The older of these two prototypes, three-year-old Saunders Roe-bodied STF 90, is operating service S between Parkhead Cross and Cardowan and was the only one of the two to be painted in Lowland's two-tone green. Lowland owned them only from March to December that year and was taken over by Scottish Omnibuses on 13 January 1958. *Geoffrey Morant*

Below: Parkhead Cross, one of the major East End shopping centres, in 1959. A crowd in Westmuir Street mills around westbound 'Coronation' tram 1238 of 1939 on service 15 from Baillieston to Anderston Cross while a pedestrian next to the pointsman's brick-built hut is engrossed in his newspaper. At first glance, this five-way junction is recognisable 44 years later, with replacement bus service 62 (and rival Stagecoach Magic Bus 162) following the same route at regular intervals. However, there has been a huge change of fortunes for the shops at the cross. Chain stores like Boots on the far left have moved into the massive Forge Shopping Centre built behind the photographer where Beardmore's Parkhead Forge steelworks stood until 1975, and these shop units have become home mostly to discount stores. A Ladbrokes betting shop has moved into the Boots unit. Parkhead Congregational Church, on the left behind the tram, was still functioning in 2003. The older building next to the parked cars has been replaced, and, although the pointsman's hut ceased to be used after routes 1 and 30 ended in March 1960 and maintained a ghostly presence long after the 15 tram finished in March 1962, phone kiosks have now taken its place. Westmuir was a mining community before the city extended eastwards. *Chris Bennett / Martin Jenkins / Online Transport Archive*

Right: Bridgeton Cross, in southeast Glasgow, was at the heart of another busy out-of-town community. This is London Road at its junction with Abercromby Street on 3 September 1962, the penultimate day of tram operation. Twenty-four-year-old 'Coronation' 1188 is maintaining the Auchenshuggle–Anderston Cross shuttle service operated for three days after bus service 64 replaced the main service 9 through to Dalmuir West. Corporation Leyland Titan PD3 and PD2 buses are following, with a Central SMT half-cab single-decker sandwiched in between. One of Central's Titan PD1s is passing on its way towards Rutherglen. *Colour-Rail*

Left: Local children, even a dog, have been attracted on to Ruby Street, outside Dalmarnock depot, the last tram depot, on 2 September 1962. Fifty trams (five 'Standards', 19 'Coronations' and 26 'Cunarders') were destroyed when fire raged through the depot in March 1961, and the building remained partially roofless until it closed. The area was comprehensively redeveloped, and a replacement bus depot opened at nearby Bridgeton in 1965. The tram, on an enthusiasts' tour, is one of the few one-offs in the standardised Glasgow fleet. No 1100 began life in 1928 as a maximum-traction 'Kilmarnock' bogie car but was rebuilt with Brill bogies within a year. Later it was rebuilt again, emerging in 1941 in the livery of the 'Coronation' cars and with similar streamlined ends grafted rather unhappily on to its original bodywork. Not repainted after 1947, it spent its latter years operating shipyard special journeys out of Partick depot. It has been at the Crich Tramway Village museum in Derbyshire since 1964. *Colour-Rail*

Below: The 18 tram from Springburn continued through Bridgeton and Dalmarnock to reach the Royal Burgh of Rutherglen and continued on to Burnside to its south. This May 1961 view — recorded two weeks before buses took over — shows a 'Coronation' with replacement flush-fitted windows crossing Rutherglen Main Street from Stonelaw Road towards Farmeloan Road on its way back to the city. Trams first served Rutherglen in April 1902. The trolleybus wires to the right of the trams brought city-bound 101s from Farmeloan Road back into Main Street on the return loop from their terminus in King Street. A thriving Clyde port in the 18th century, Rutherglen became a Royal burgh in 1126 — 49 years before Glasgow was granted its burgh charter — and remained independent until local-government reorganisation added it to Glasgow in 1975, along with neighbouring Cambuslang. It was separated again from the city in 1996, when it became part of the new South Lanarkshire Council. *Colour-Rail*

Left: Corporation buses were extended into the huge new south-Glasgow housing scheme at Castlemilk, on the edge of the hilly Cathkin Braes just across the boundary from Rutherglen, in 1956. The area takes its name from a house built there *c*1460, when the Stuart family relocated from their original Castlemilk House in Dumfries-shire. In this June 1971 view, forward-entrance Leyland Titan PD3/2 72-seaters L377 of 1960 and, behind it, L364 of 1962, set down passengers in Castlemilk Drive, near the end of their journey on service 46 from the equally large east-Glasgow scheme at Easterhouse. Service 46 still operates. It doesn't go into the city centre, but runs via once-busy Bridgeton. A shorter version began in 1954 between Cranhill and Croftfoot. Although they look almost identical, Alexander bodied L377 at Falkirk, while Corporation employees assembled the bodywork on L364 at the Coplawhill tramcar works from Alexander parts. When new, these buses had unusual Leyland-Albion badges on the front, and, although the oval Albion badge, with Scottish Saltire flag, has fallen off L377, it is still on L364. *Murdoch Currie*

Below: While most other routes in the area were extended to Castlemilk in 1956, the 13 via the High Street to the Edinburgh Road housing estates at Greenfield and Lightburn continued to terminate at Croftfoot, the inter-war suburb directly to the north. B107, a 1950 Albion Venturer emerging from Thorncroft Drive into Croftfoot Road in May 1962, was built entirely in Greater Glasgow — its Albion chassis in Scotstoun and its Brockhouse body in Clydebank. It is in a hybrid livery typical of several buses partially repainted at Parkhead garage, with bottom half in the yellow-and-narrow-cream-band style introduced in 1959 and the top in the previous style of green with cream roof. A few buses were painted the other way round, with green top half and old-style orange and cream below. *Iain MacGregor*

Below: Trolleybuses ran south as far as Muirend from August 1952 and over the boundary to Clarkston from July 1953. Service 104 from Cathedral Street replaced the Adelphi Street–Muirend section of motor bus 37, but it became the first significant route to be abandoned when it was axed without a direct replacement on 6 January 1962. On the route's final day, Sunbeam F4A TG3 turns from Clarkston Road into Muirend Road, with the 1933 Toledo cinema visible above the brick workshop on the left. The Toledo — built by William Beresford Inglis, later responsible for the art deco Beresford Hotel at Charing Cross — only closed in recent years after many earlier threats to its future. The dairy on the left has gone, replaced by a Safeway supermarket. TG3 was new in 1953 and was one of only five Alexander-bodied trolleybuses ever built for revenue-earning service. All 20 Sunbeams were classified as TG rather than TS, as the Corporation only used 'S' to identify its single-deck buses; the 'G' stood for Guy, Sunbeam's owner. *Iain MacGregor*

Right: The 104 and 105 trolleybuses reached Muirend and Clarkston via Mount Florida, travelling along Cathcart Road from the right. This is May 1951, a year before trolleybuses appeared here. A 'Standard' tram on the 13 from Milngavie, beyond the city's northwestern boundary, is about to meet 'Standard' 463 (new 1903 and withdrawn 1958) as it prepares to take up peak hour duty on the short inter-suburban 12 route to Paisley Road Toll, Govan and Linthouse. When trolleybus 108 replaced the 12 in November 1958, it was the last occasion when trolleybuses replaced trams anywhere in the British Isles. Tram 463 is in Holmlea Road, with Langside depot behind. This closed in 1956, reopened as a bus garage in 1957 and closed permanently in 1984; the site has since been redeveloped as flats. *W. J. Wyse collection / LRTA London Area*

Below right: LS31, the Corporation's first postwar one-man-operated bus, ended its first day in service — 9 May 1965 — on the end of a towbar behind AEC Matador breakdown lorry FYS 10. This 36ft-long Alexander-bodied Leyland Panther — with rear engine, two doors, 42 seats and standing room for another 31 passengers — was involved in a minor accident partway through its first shift on the short south-side route 40 between Cathcart and Peat Road, Pollok, and was being taken back to the Larkfield bus works for repairs. All 16 of the Corporation's Panthers were painted in similar style to the 'upside-down' scheme tried briefly in 1964, as was one Worldmaster kept as a spare one-man bus. This embarrassing procession is turning from Queen's Drive into Victoria Road, with the gates to Queen's Park behind. Queen's Park, with its spectacular views north across the city, opened in September 1862 — Queen Victoria's Silver Jubilee year. While Victoria Road clearly honours that queen, the park isn't hers but is named in honour of Mary Queen of Scots, who fled Scotland after losing the Battle of Langside (on lands now occupied by the park) in May 1568. *Ian Maclean*

Left: Tradeston, due south of the city centre, lies to the west of the riverside communities of Laurieston and Hutchesontown, better known to many outside the city as the Gorbals; this was the equivalent of New York's Lower East Side, being the place where immigrants first set up home, and by the 1930s housed 65,000 people in often overcrowded conditions. This 1956 view at Tradeston shows five-year-old 'Cunarder' tram 1386 — still with its original half-drop upper-deck front windows — about to turn to its right from Commerce Street into Nelson Street on its way from Anniesland to Elderslie via Paisley, having crossed the Clyde by the King George V Bridge, opened in 1928. Visible in the distance is the tower of Glasgow Central station. Service 21 was withdrawn when Glasgow Corporation abandoned all of its Paisley-area routes in May 1957. Modern low-rise industrial premises have long since replaced the buildings behind. *Frank Hunt collection / LRTA London Area*

Below: This is the same junction, looking west along Nelson Street *c*1959. The tramlines have been lifted, the road is being resurfaced, and BUT trolleybus TB69 is travelling east under the westbound overhead to get around the obstruction. It is on service 106 from Bellahouston to Millerston — at almost 10 miles the longest of all the trolleybus services. The 106 required 55 vehicles, and, although this was as close as it got to the city centre, it linked the shipyards and docks of Govan with heavily populated Gorbals, Bridgeton and Dennistoun. It began in June 1958, replacing 'yellow' tram 7 — a route known to crews as the 'Yellow Peril' because the sheer number of short-distance passengers provided conductors with some of the busiest shifts on the system. Bus 65 replaced the 106 in October 1966, but it's some sign of how Glasgow has changed that there is no equivalent route 37 years later. The signpost to the left, with coloured stripes to identify the different docks, was one of many used to help lorry drivers find their way around the riverside communities.
Ian Maclean

Prince's Dock, on the southern bank of the Clyde, opened in 1897, substantially increasing the cargo-handling capacity of Glasgow's harbour and complementing the two-basin Queen's Dock on the north side of the river. Queen's Dock closed in 1969, Prince's Dock a few years later. The Scottish Exhibition & Conference Centre stands on the site of the former, while the filled-in Prince's Dock — since renamed Pacific Quay — was home to the 1988 Garden Festival, when trams ran again here for the first (and, so far, only) time since 1962. The Glasgow Science Centre has since opened on part of the site, and BBC Scotland plans to relocate here from the Botanic Gardens. In this January 1962 view, Western SMT JD2174, a 1950 all-Leyland Titan PD2/1 acquired almost

new with the Young's business, is following Govan Road and the trolleybus overhead for service 106 as it swings sharply around the dock's three deep-sea basins. The National Dock Labour Board offices on the corner of Mavisbank Road have long since gone the way of Glasgow's stevedores, and that part of the site has been over-planted with trees. The 1894 Clyde Navigation Trust building to the left survives and in 2003 was home to the Beat 106FM radio station. Also preserved as a monument to a bygone industrial age is the hammerhead Finnieston Crane (pronounced 'cran' by locals) on the north bank, which used to lift Glasgow-built steam locomotives onto ships for export.
Iain MacGregor

Govan, with a population of 91,000, was the fifth-largest Scottish burgh when Glasgow absorbed it in November 1912, ending 48 years of independence. This ancient community became a Christian settlement in 565AD and expanded rapidly in the 19th century to become one of the centres of shipbuilding. Govan Cross also became a public-transport interchange, when its Subway station opened in 1896, connecting with horse trams between Linthouse to the west and the city centre. Such was Govan's importance as a shopping, employment and entertainment centre that Corporation bus services also developed from here to newer south-side housing estates. Two private operators from the Paisley area ran half-hourly services to Govan Cross. First to reach here, in 1958, were the blue buses of Renfrew-based Paton Bros, on a service from Paisley and Renfrew Airport. The orange buses of Hawkhead-based Graham's Bus Service followed in 1963, running from Linwood (where the Hillman Imp

car was made), Paisley and Penilee. Both terminated at the north end of Helen Street, directly round the block from the subway station in Greenhaugh Street. When Paton's took advantage of Government grants and started buying new buses in 1970, these vehicles usually started out on the Govan route. This is February 1974, with a new Willowbrook-bodied Leyland Leopard of Paton's standing ahead of Graham's Leyland Atlantean L3. The Graham's bus — the only low-height Atlantean supplied to a Scottish operator — was new in 1971, but its Alexander body was built on a 1967 PDR1/3 chassis. Western SMT bought the Paton business in August 1979, while Graham's closed down in April 1990. The Helen Street tenements were demolished c1977, and the Govan bus station and Subway station were constructed here three years later.
Brian Deans

Two Corporation bus routes ran from Govan Cross to Hillington Industrial Estate, opened in 1940 as a focus for new industries. Some of these industries (like Rolls-Royce aero engines) took advantage of the shadow-factory programme to scatter strategically essential production around Britain and minimise the impact of enemy air attacks. Until May 1964 a low railway bridge over Hillington Road impeded access to the southern end of the estate, so most of the Corporation's single-deckers were kept to operate the 25 from Govan Cross, shuttle service 27 from Birkhall Avenue, at Paisley Road West, and the 40 from Cathcart. Eventually the bridge was replaced and the road beneath was lowered to accommodate double-deckers. This is February 1964 and work on the bridge is well advanced as 1952 Daimler CVD6 DS33 — with dual-door body built in the Corporation's Larkfield bus works — heads towards Govan. The bodywork on these 43 buses was built between 1948 and 1952 and shared some design features with that of the 'Cunarder' trams built at the same time. Eighteen had been taken out of service by 1963, and removal of the Hillington Road bridge ended the careers of the other 25 and of nine newer Leyland Worldmasters. *Iain MacGregor*

The southern terminus of Glasgow's first tram route was at Eglinton Toll (or St Andrew's Cross, as the builders of the tenement building above the Star Bar called it), one mile south of the city centre. Until 18 August 1946 it was a conventional junction where Pollokshaws Road crossed between the ends of Eglinton Street and Victoria Road. Then the barrier in the foreground was erected, cutting Pollokshaws Road in half and removing the direct connection between Victoria Road and Eglinton Street. Five tram and five bus routes changed that day. This is April 1960 and tram 1220 — a 1938 'Coronation' with replacement bodywork built in 1942 — is turning from Eglinton Street into Maxwell Road on service 3 from Park Road to Mosspark while a Western

SMT Leyland Titan PD3 heads along Pollokshaws Road on its way from Clyde Street to Eaglesham. The 3 was to have been Glasgow's last tram route, but the bridge over the railway in Maxwell Road needed to be replaced as part of the south-side 'Blue Train' electrification project, so it came off in June 1960, two years and three months before final service 9. Replacement bus 59 was routed along Albert Drive rather than Maxwell Road, which has since been closed off at this end. The Star Bar survives 43 years later, and First Glasgow drivers from nearby Larkfield depot frequently come on and off duty at the bus stop on the Eglinton Street side of the bar. A monumental mason's yard occupies the site of the newer industrial buildings beyond. *Colour-Rail*

Albert Drive, in the small East Pollokshields industrial zone, was at the very heart of the tramway system. Coplawhill Works, which built most and overhauled all of the trams, was here. So was the motor school, where drivers were trained, and the permanent-way yard was in adjacent Barrland Street. Coplawhill became Glasgow's first transport museum in 1964 and reopened in 1989 as the Tramway Theatre. The motor school also trained bus drivers for south-side garages, although its buses were kept at Larkfield garage, in nearby Victoria Road. Here, AEC Regent AR287 prepares to take up training duties outside St Ninian's Episcopal Church, next door to Coplawhill Works. This was one of the Corporation's longest-lasting buses: when new in 1938 as bus 612, it had Cowieson bodywork built within the city at Charles Street, Garngad;

it assumed its later identity when the replacement Crossley body was supplied in 1951 and served as a training bus between 1959 and 1966, its clutch and manual 'crash' gearbox making it useful for those drivers who required a full PSV driving licence. It survived long enough to be painted in the post-1959 livery style — even if one of its upper-deck windows had disappeared by the time this picture was taken — but was scrapped before the Scottish bus-preservation movement was big enough to save such a significant vehicle. Ten of these buses were originally to have had their replacement bodywork built at Townhead by the Crossley agent, Scottish Commercial, but only one was built in Glasgow, and Crossley assembled the other nine in Stockport, using a mix of its own and its agent's parts. *Ian Maclean*

When trolleybus service 108 replaced the venerable 'Standard' trams on the short service 12 between Paisley Road Toll and Mount Florida in November 1958 the route became home to the 10 longest buses in Britain. Although the national length limit was 30ft and another three years were to pass before this was increased to 36ft, the Corporation obtained Ministry of Transport dispensation to operate these 34ft 6in BUT RETB1s with 50-seat Burlingham single-deck bodywork built in Blackpool. End-to-end journey time was just 18min, although peak-period 108s took another 17min on the extension beyond Paisley Road Toll to Linthouse and Shieldhall to carry shipyard workers.

This 1965 picture shows TBS12, numerically the first of these pioneering buses, passing Shields Road station while the railway bridge was being reconstructed to accommodate the Glasgow–Gourock/Wemyss Bay electrification work. The southbound trolleybus wires have been temporarily relocated closer to the northbound overhead while this work is undertaken. Electric 'Blue Trains' began running through Shields Road in June 1967 (three months after double-deck motor-bus service 68 replaced the trolleybuses), but the station closed in February 1966. TBS12 was scrapped, but similar TBS13 is displayed in Glasgow's transport museum. *Ian Maclean*

Below: This is Nithsdale Road, where Pollokshields meets the smaller suburb of Dumbreck. It's 30 April 1960, and 'Coronation' tram 1395 — one of six built as recently as 1954 — is heading back to the city on service 3. This route, always electrified and usually operated with the Corporation's newest trams of the day, served the large Victorian villas and prosperous 'carriage folk' of leafy Pollokshields. Often, it also passed the ornamental lamp-posts that marked out the residence of a serving Lord Provost (Scottish equivalent of Lord Mayor). No wonder that, when the 3 came off a month after this picture was taken, an article by Ian Coonie in *The Modern Tramway* described it as 'the route of the high and mighty'. He argued that its existence should 'dispel the Londoner's idea that trams are proletarian vehicles never found where the best people live'. The bridge spans the Paisley Canal railway line, opened in 1885 on the filled-in Glasgow, Paisley, Johnstone & Ardrossan Canal, built 1806-11 and which only ever reached Elderslie. Passenger services on the line ceased in 1983 but resumed in 1990 with a new station — Dumbreck — here on the right-hand side of Nithsdale Road. A second bridge, nearer the camera, was built in the 1990s over the new M77 motorway, taking away some of the gardens in the foreground of this picture. *Colour-Rail*

Right: In August 1923 the 'white' tram that later became service 3 was extended from Dumbreck to serve new council housing at Mosspark. Most of the 1¼-mile extension took trams along this private reservation on the north side of Mosspark Boulevard, next to Bellahouston Park. Fifteen years later, during a particularly rain-soaked summer, the park was home to the last prewar Empire Exhibition, and trams carried many of the 12.5 million visitors. Miraculously, the Boulevard wasn't widened when the tram tracks were lifted — just grassed over, with ghostly traces of its former role where it meets up with paved surfaces. This April 1960 view shows 'Coronation' 1393, the first of the last six new trams built in 1954. Coplawhill Works reverted to its prewar design, simplified by flush-mounted glazing and the omission of a driver's cab door, when it built these trams on trucks bought second-hand from Liverpool, where they had been salvaged after a major fire. Fire played a big part in their short lives, for they replaced fire-damaged 'Coronations' and four of the six — including 1393 and 1395 in the picture below — were lost in the Dalmarnock depot fire in March 1961. *Colour-Rail*

This is the north side of Bellahouston Park in 1958. Tram 1001, hired by enthusiasts, is in Jura Street, just north of Paisley Road West, and the obelisk in the park behind commemorates the visit of King George VI and Queen Elizabeth to the Empire Exhibition site in 1937. Most of the exhibition buildings were temporary structures, including the Atlantic restaurant, built around the obelisk in the style of an ocean liner. Only the Palace of Art (now a sports hall) survives. Tram 1001 was one of five four-wheel lightweights built between 1939 and 1942 with a view to finding a cheaper replacement for the trusty old 'Standard' double-deckers. They were scrapped after Govan depot lost its trams in November 1958 and, like many non-standard cars, ended their days on shipyard specials. The line from Craigton Road to Bellahouston opened in February 1938, extending the 'Yellow Peril' service 7 and, for the duration of the exhibition, from May to October that year, carried special service 31 from the Whiteinch Ferry at Linthouse. Trolleybus 106 also terminated in Jura Street, but replacement bus 65 was cut back to Craigton (actually Ibrox bus garage) in September 1974, when construction work began on the M8 motorway just north of here. *A. P. Tatt*

Right: Whether they were buses, trolleybuses or trams, few Corporation single-deckers led long or successful lives, and Leyland Panther LS33 had one of the briefest of all careers. With big panoramic windows in its Alexander W-type body, it was one of the star attractions of the 1967 Scottish Motor Show in the Kelvin Hall, yet it operated only from February 1968 until 1971 and was scrapped four years later. This photograph was taken in Braidcraft Road, Pollok, when it was in only its third week of operation on service 21 to Midland Street; it was one of six buses by then available for the two or three one-man-operated duties on this service. Although experimental one-man operation of the 21 began in August 1965, national wage agreements prevented the Corporation from dispensing with conductors on this and parallel service 39 until February 1969, by which time Atlantean double-deckers were proving to be more reliable than the 16 Panthers bought for these routes. Together with neighbouring Nitshill, Househillwood and Priesthill, Pollok was developed in the 1930s and 1940s on land bought in 1926 from Sir John Stirling-Maxwell, whose Nether Pollok Estate had already developed the villas and low-rise tenements of Pollokshields. He tried in vain to persuade the Corporation's housing department to develop this, one of the city's large peripheral housing schemes, as a high-quality garden suburb. *Iain MacGregor*

Right: The southernmost of the Pollok-area housing schemes, South Nitshill was built on the Darnley Estate fields (to the right of the picture) after this section of the Paisley tram system closed in September 1956. This is shortly before the end, with 1949-built 'Cunarder' 1306 speeding out of Barrhead by Parkhouse Road on a service 14 journey from Cross Stobs to the University. It is about to enter the private light railway from here to Spiersbridge, opened in 1910, when Paisley District Tramways was a private company. The 14 survived until November 1959, cut back to terminate at Arden (pronounced in true Glasgow vernacular with the emphasis on the second syllable, to sound like the Belgian Ardennes). Construction of South Nitshill began in 1957, and Corporation buses were restored to this southern extremity in June 1961. Forty-two years later, much of the housing is demolished, leaving a ghostly pattern of empty streets. *Frank Hunt collection / LRTA London Area*

Index of Locations

Albert Bridge	11	Dumbreck	76	Partick	49
Anderston	37, 38	Dundas Street	30, 32	Pollok	79
Anniesland	47, 48	Eglinton Toll	73	Pollokshields	5, 74, 75, 76
Argyle Street	Title page, 20, 37, 38	George Square	6, 7	Prince's Dock	70
Bath Street	24	Glasgow Bridge	18	Queen's Park	67
Bellahouston Park	77, 78	Glasgow Cross	8, 9	Renfield Street	23
Botanic Gardens	44, 45	Govan	71	Renfrew Street	Back cover
Bothwell Street	39	Great Western Road	4, 44, 45, 46, 47, 48	Royston	58
Bridgegate	13	High Street	9, 10	Rutherglen	63
Bridgeton	61	Hillington	72	St Enoch	15, 16
Broomielaw	17	Hope Street	21	Sauchiehall Street	21
Buchanan Street	26, 27, 28, 29	Hyndland Road	46	Scotstoun	50, 51
Castlemilk	64	Jamaica Street	Front cover, 18, 19	Shettleston	59
Charing Cross	3, 40, 41	Kelvin Hall	42	South Nitshill	79
Clyde Street	12, 14, 15	Kelvingrove	42, 43	Tradeston	68, 69
Cowcaddens	23	Keppochhill Road	57	Union Street	22
Croftfoot	65	Maryhill	54, 55, 56	Victoria Bridge	13
Cunningham Street	33	Mosspark	77	Waterloo Street	36
Dalmarnock	62	Mount Florida	67	Wellington Street	37
Dalmuir	52, 53	Muirend	66	West Nile Street	24, 25
Dennistoun	58	Parkhead	60		
Dumbarton Road	42, 43, 49, 50	Parliamentary Road	30, 31, 34, 35		

Front cover: A Corporation tram and bus in Jamaica Street in the late-1950s. 'Coronation' tram 1242, on former 'white car' service 3 to Pollokshields and Mosspark, was new in January 1939 and lasted until June 1962. Metro-Cammell-bodied AEC Regent III A159, on route 43 from Kelvinside to Cathcart, was new in March 1950 and was sold for scrap in June 1968. Bus 43 replaced tram service 5 in November 1957. *Jim Thomson*

Back cover: Alexander (Midland) Albion Lowlander MRE24 in Renfrew Street, just east of Cambridge Street, in May 1966. It is nearing the end of its journey from Milngavie via Anniesland and Great Western Road and is being followed by two Corporation buses — an AEC Regent V on the 20 from Drumchapel to George Square and a Daimler CVG6 on the 2 from Knightswood to Rutherglen. The Camp Bar is an example of a widespread practice of the time and a by-product of licensing laws, as the tenements above have been demolished but the pub lives on. The Thistle Hotel has risen to occupy this site. *Iain MacGregor*